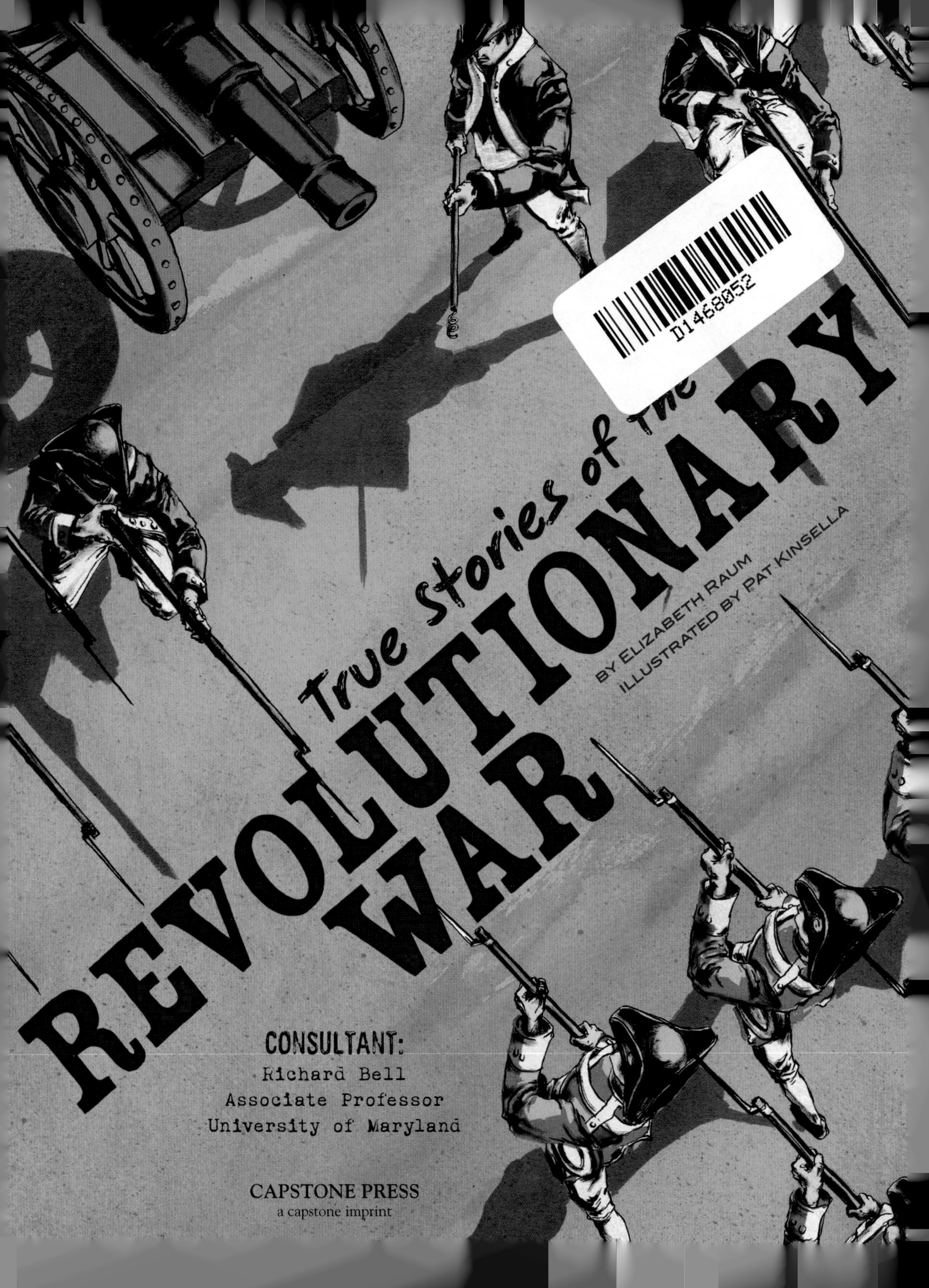

True Stories of the REVOLUTIONARY WAR

by Elizabeth Raum

illustrated by Pat Kinsella

CONSULTANT:

Richard Bell

Associate Professor

University of Maryland

CAPSTONE PRESS

a capstone imprint

Graphic Library is published by Capstone Press,
1710 Roe Crest Drive,
North Mankato, Minnesota 56003.
www.capstonepub.com

Library of Congress Cataloging-in-Publication Data
Raum, Elizabeth.
True stories of the Revolutionary War / by Elizabeth Raum;
illustrated by Pat Kinsella.
p. cm. — (Graphic library. Stories of war)
Includes index.
Summary: "In graphic novel format, tells the stories of
six men and women who fought for their beliefs during the
Revolutionary War"—Provided by publisher.
ISBN 978-1-4296-8674-7 (library binding)
ISBN 978-1-4296-9342-4 (paperback)
ISBN 978-1-62065-269-5 (ebook PDF)
1. United States—History—Revolution, 1775-1783—Biography—
Juvenile literature. 2. United States—History—Revolution,
1775-1783—Comic books, strips, etc.—Juvenile literature.
I. Kinsella, Pat, ill. II. Title.
E206.R38 2013
973.3—dc23   2012003965

EDITOR: Jill Kalz

DESIGNER: Ashlee Suker

ART DIRECTOR: Nathan Gassman

PRODUCTION SPECIALIST: Laura Manthe

Editor's note: Direct quotations from primary sources are indicated by yellow text.

Direct quotations appear on the following pages:
Page 7 from the Declaration of Independence.
Pages 11, 13, 19, 20 from *Narratives of the American Revolution* by Hugh F. Rankin, ed. (Chicago:
    R. R. Donnelley & Sons, 1976).
Pages 23, 25 from *Diary of Lieutenant Anthony Allaire* by Anthony Allaire (New York: New York
    Times & Arno Press, 1968).
Pages 28, 29 from "Eyewitness Account at Yorktown of Sarah Osborn Benjamin" by David N. Moran
    (http://www.revolutionarywararchives.org/battles-link/73-eyewitness-account-at-yorktown-of-
    sarah-osborn-benjamin).

Photo credits: illustration background by Jon Proctor, 2, 4, 30-31

Printed in the United States of America in Stevens Point, Wisconsin.
062014   008322R

TABLE OF CONTENTS

CHAPTER 1
The American Revolution:
A War for Independence 4

CHAPTER 2
Isaac Bangs: The Declaration of Independence 6

CHAPTER 3
Frederika von Riedesel:
The Battle of Freeman's Farm 10

CHAPTER 4
Lydia Darragh: Spying in Philadelphia 14

CHAPTER 5
Albigence Waldo: The Battle of White Marsh 18

CHAPTER 6
Lieutenant Anthony Allaire:
The Battle of Monck's Corner 22

CHAPTER 7
Sarah Osborn Benjamin:
The Battle of Yorktown 26

Glossary 30
Read More 31
Internet Sites 31
Index 32

THE AMERICAN REVOLUTION: A WAR FOR INDEPENDENCE

Since the founding of Jamestown, Virginia, in 1607, England ruled much of colonial America. And for more than 150 years, life was generally good. Most colonists considered themselves English. They spoke English, practiced English manners, and traded with England.

During the 1750s, war broke out between France and Great Britain. The French and Indian War (1754–1763) left Great Britain in need of money. King George III forced American colonists to pay new taxes to cover the war costs. The Stamp Act, passed in 1765, taxed most printed materials, including newspapers, stamps, and even playing cards. Many colonists refused to pay. They thought it unfair that they should have to pay these taxes, yet have no direct say in their government. Eventually the Stamp Act was overturned. Colonists also decided to boycott, or stop buying, British products, such as tea. When a large shipment of tea arrived in Boston Harbor, tempers flared. Angry colonists in Boston snuck onto the three tea ships one night and dumped 90,000 pounds (40,820 kilograms) of tea into Boston Harbor.

Anger rose quickly throughout the colonies. Fighting broke out between the colonists and British soldiers on April 19, 1775, at Lexington and Concord, Massachusetts. A little more than a year later, on July 4, 1776, the colonies declared their independence from Great Britain.

More than 200,000 colonists fought in the Revolutionary War. Unlike the British soldiers, many were woefully untrained. They often lacked guns, ammunition, and other basic supplies. But despite the odds, after eight long years, the patriots won their freedom.

Throughout the war, people wrote letters and kept diaries and journals about their daily lives. Thanks to the writings of the six men and women in this book, you can hear the cries of battle. You can smell the gunpowder, and feel the fear and bravery inside the true stories of the Revolutionary War.

KEY DATES

APRIL 1775: Shots are fired at Lexington and Concord (Massachusetts).

JUNE 1775: The Battle of Bunker Hill (Breeds Hill; Massachusetts) is the first battle of the Revolutionary War.

JULY 4, 1776: The Continental Congress adopts the Declaration of Independence.

AUGUST 1776: The British win the Battle of Long Island (New York).

SEPTEMBER – OCTOBER 1777: The Battles at Saratoga (New York) strengthen the Continental Army's confidence.

DECEMBER 1777: The Continental Army reaches Valley Forge (Pennsylvania).

APRIL 1780: The British win the Battle of Monck's Corner (South Carolina).

MARCH 15, 1781: The British win the Battle of Guilford Courthouse (North Carolina).

SEPTEMBER – OCTOBER 1781: The Continental Army wins the Battle of Yorktown (Virginia), the final major land battle of the war.

FEBRUARY 14, 1783: Great Britain officially declares an end to the war.

SEPTEMBER 3, 1783: The United States and Great Britain sign the Treaty of Paris.

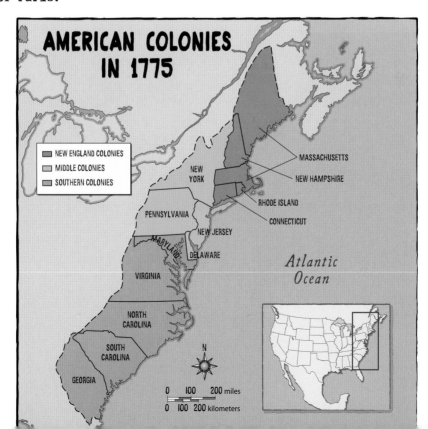

AMERICAN COLONIES IN 1775

NEW ENGLAND COLONIES
MIDDLE COLONIES
SOUTHERN COLONIES

MASSACHUSETTS
NEW HAMPSHIRE
RHODE ISLAND
CONNECTICUT
NEW YORK
PENNSYLVANIA
NEW JERSEY
MARYLAND
DELAWARE
VIRGINIA
NORTH CAROLINA
SOUTH CAROLINA
GEORGIA

Atlantic Ocean

N

0   100   200 miles
0   100   200 kilometers

CH. 2

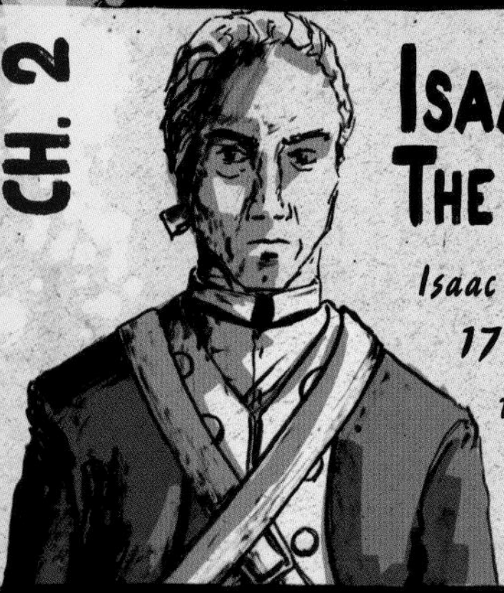

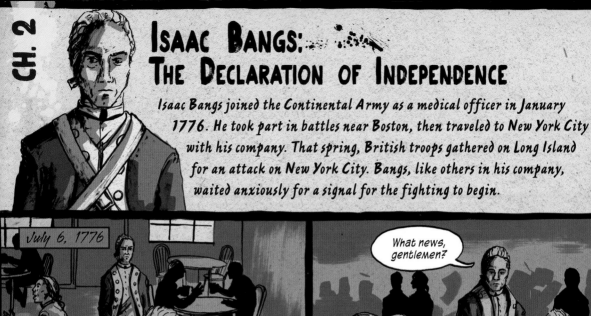

Isaac Bangs: The Declaration of Independence

Isaac Bangs joined the Continental Army as a medical officer in January 1776. He took part in battles near Boston, then traveled to New York City with his company. That spring, British troops gathered on Long Island for an attack on New York City. Bangs, like others in his company, waited anxiously for a signal for the fighting to begin.

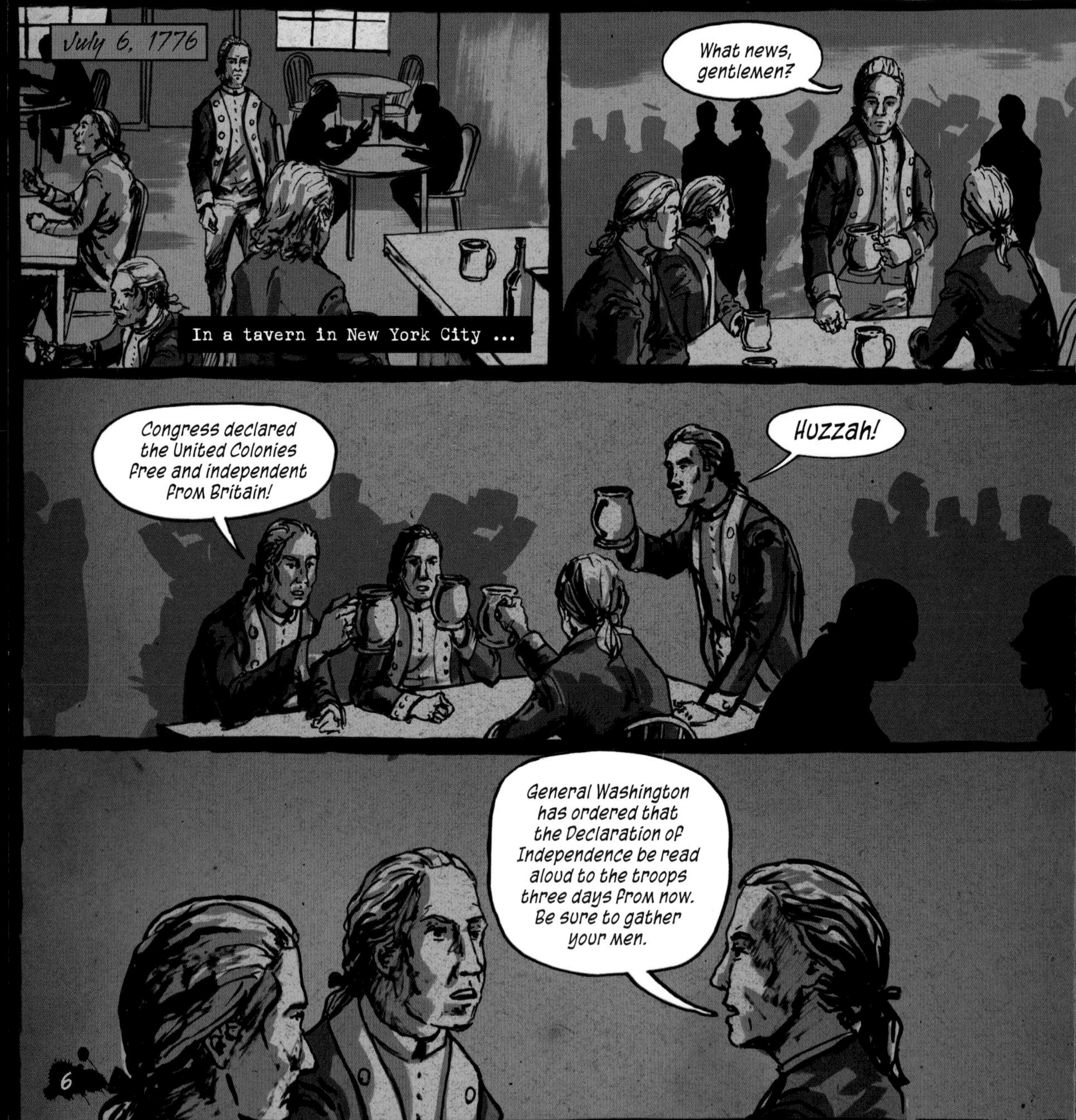

July 6, 1776
In a tavern in New York City ...
What news, gentlemen?
Congress declared the United Colonies free and independent from Britain!
Huzzah!
General Washington has ordered that the Declaration of Independence be read aloud to the troops three days from now. Be sure to gather your men.

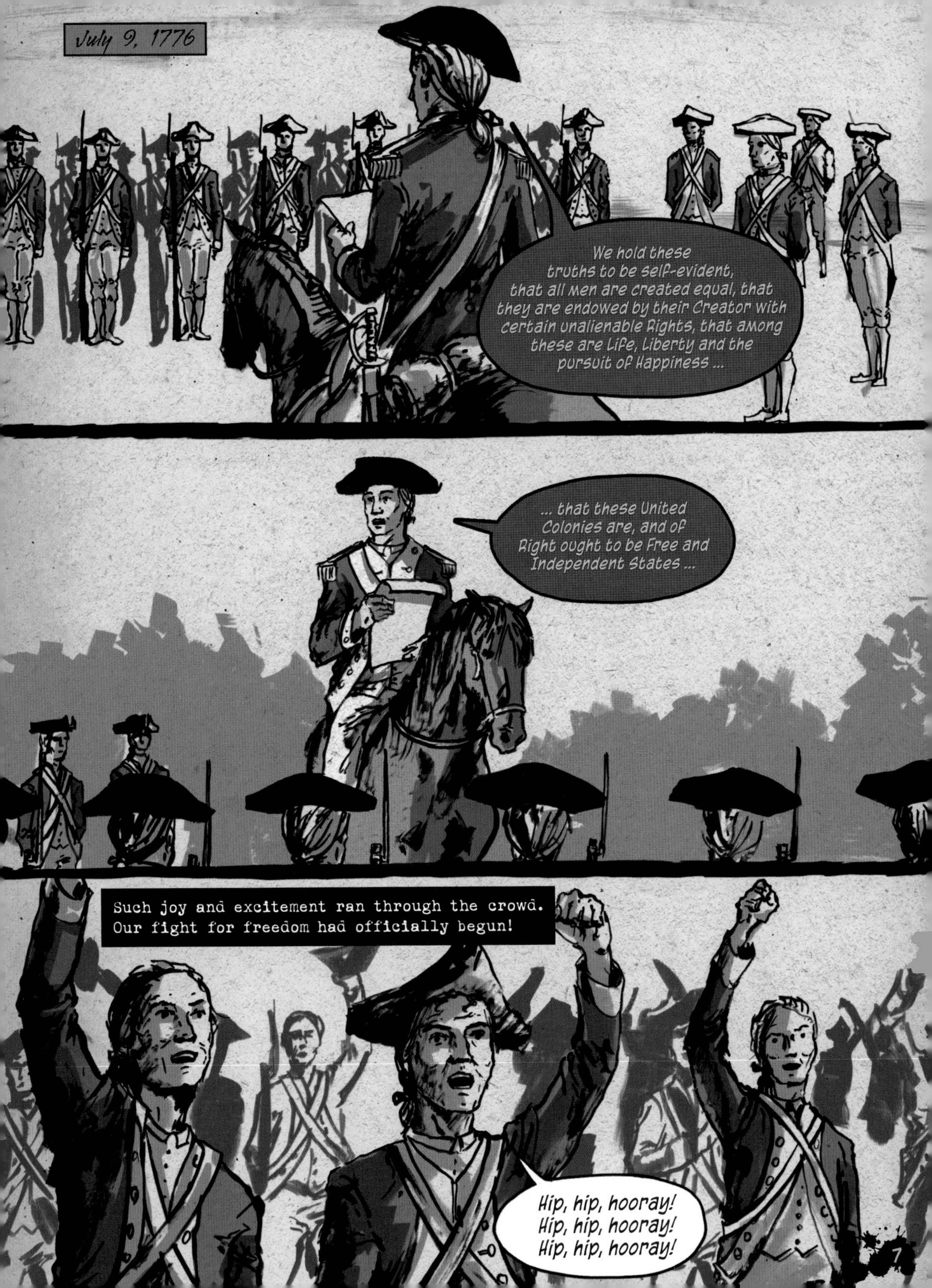
July 9, 1776
We hold these truths to be self-evident, that all men are created equal, that they are endowed by their Creator with certain unalienable Rights, that among these are Life, Liberty and the pursuit of Happiness ...
... that these United Colonies are, and of Right ought to be Free and Independent States ...
Such joy and excitement ran through the crowd. Our fight for freedom had officially begun!
Hip, hip, hooray! Hip, hip, hooray! Hip, hip, hooray!

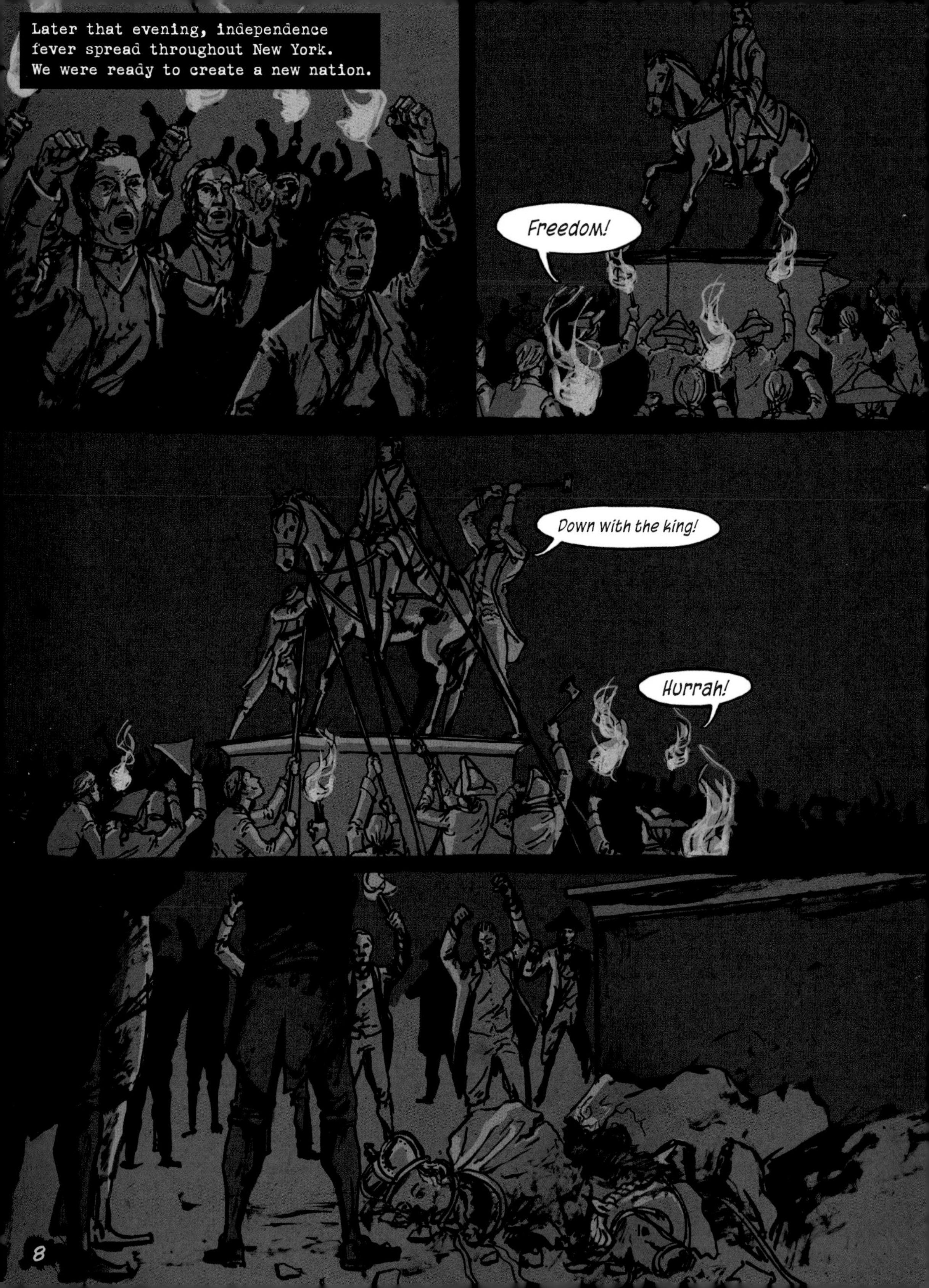
Later that evening, independence fever spread throughout New York. We were ready to create a new nation.
Freedom!
Down with the king!
Hurrah!

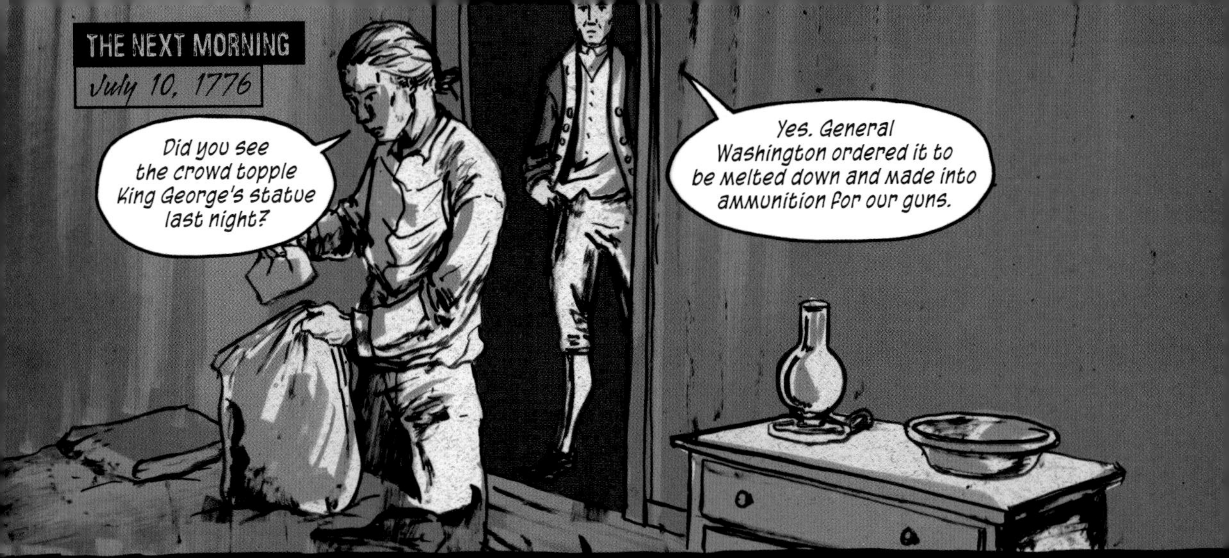
THE NEXT MORNING
July 10, 1776
Did you see the crowd topple King George's statue last night?
Yes. General Washington ordered it to be melted down and made into ammunition for our guns.

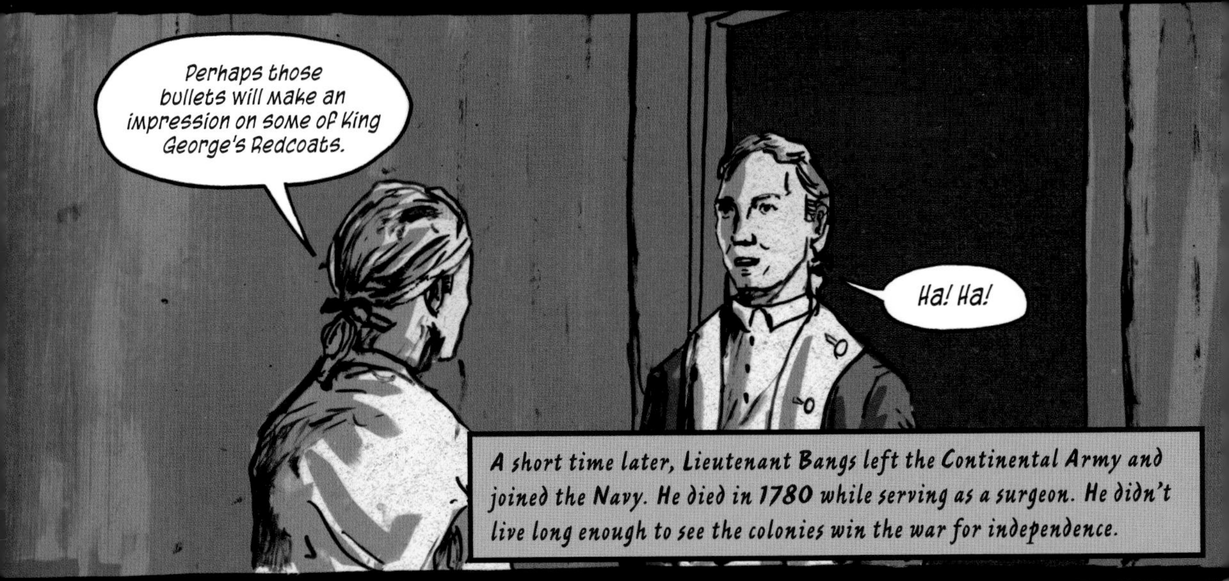
Perhaps those bullets will make an impression on some of King George's Redcoats.
Ha! Ha!
A short time later, Lieutenant Bangs left the Continental Army and joined the Navy. He died in 1780 while serving as a surgeon. He didn't live long enough to see the colonies win the war for independence.

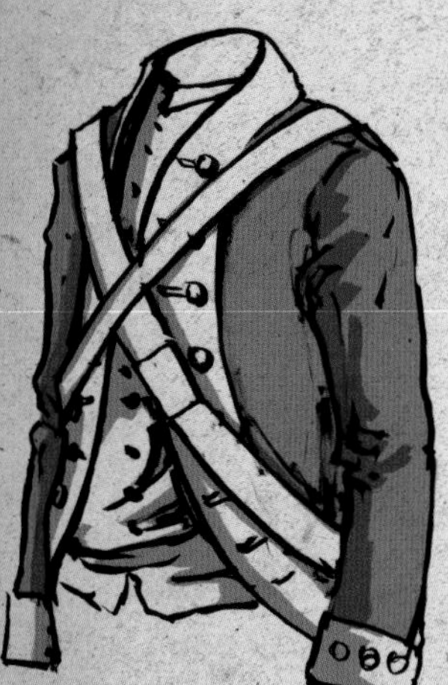

REDCOATS

American colonists called British soldiers Redcoats because they wore bright red coats and white breeches (short pants). General Washington and his officers wore deep blue coats and buff-colored breeches. Every regiment designed its own special coat buttons.

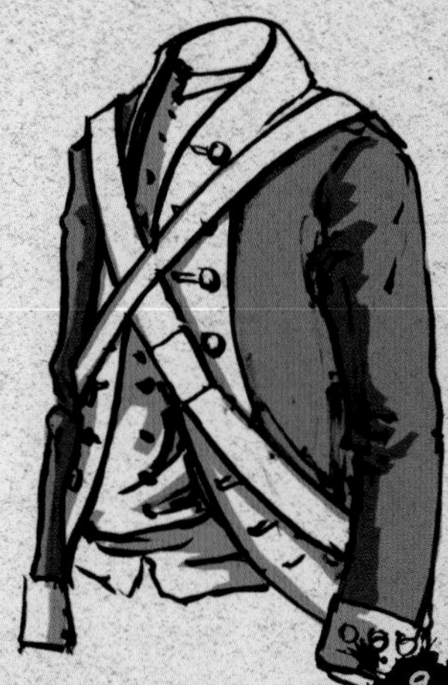

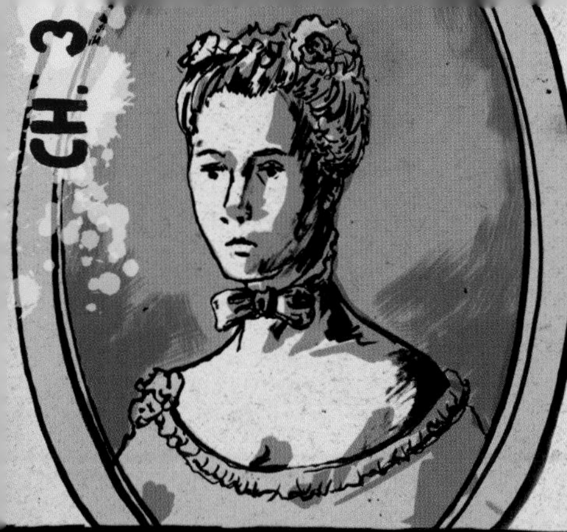

Frederika von Riedesel: The Battle of Freeman's Farm

In 1777 Baroness Frederika von Riedesel came to America from Germany. Her husband, a German general, commanded German soldiers fighting with the British. Frederika brought along three young daughters and several servants. They joined General von Riedesel in Canada and began following the British army south through New York.

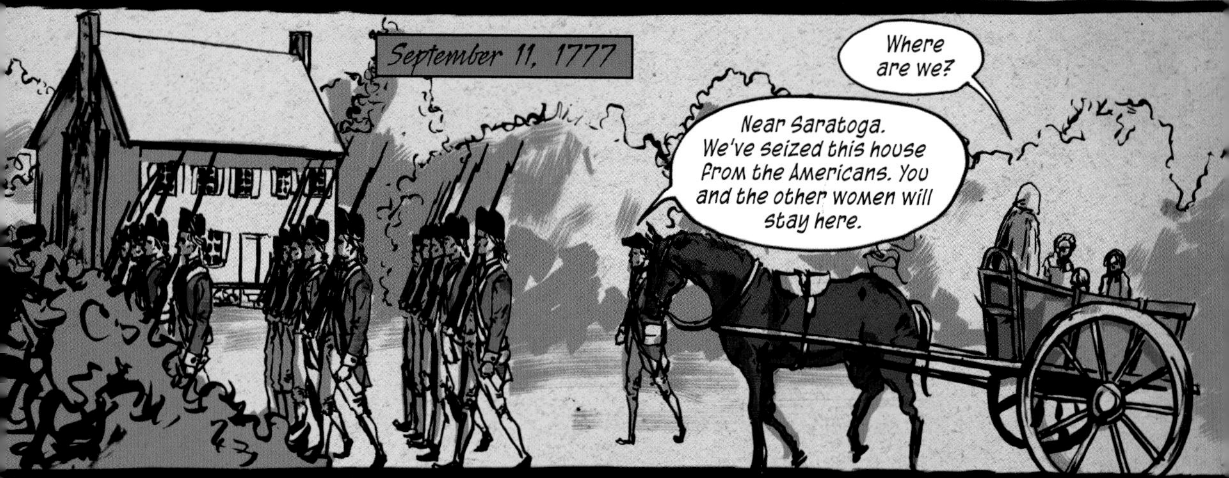
September 11, 1777
Where are we?
Near Saratoga. We've seized this house from the Americans. You and the other women will stay here.

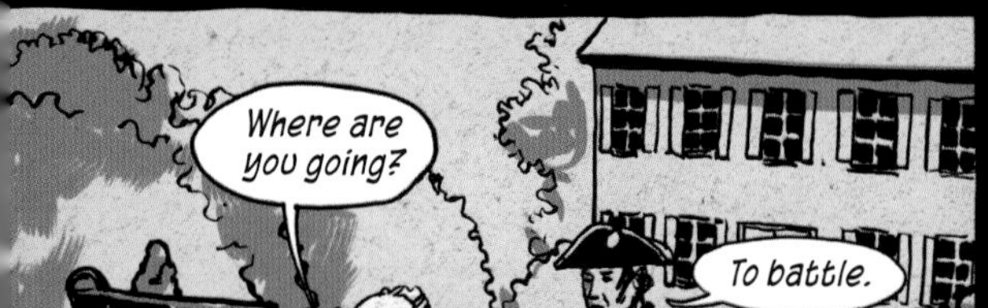
Where are you going?
To battle.

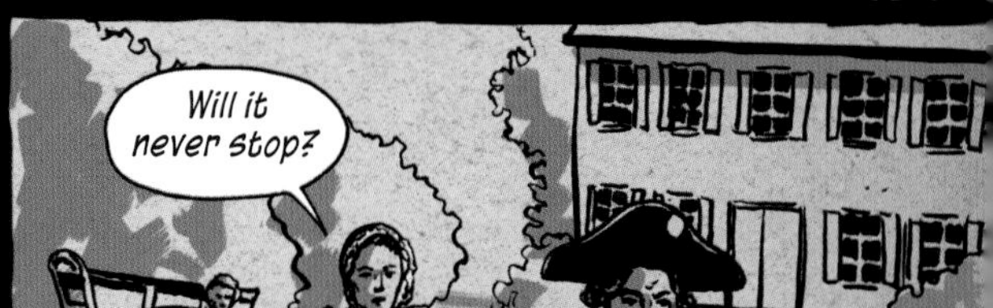
Will it never stop?

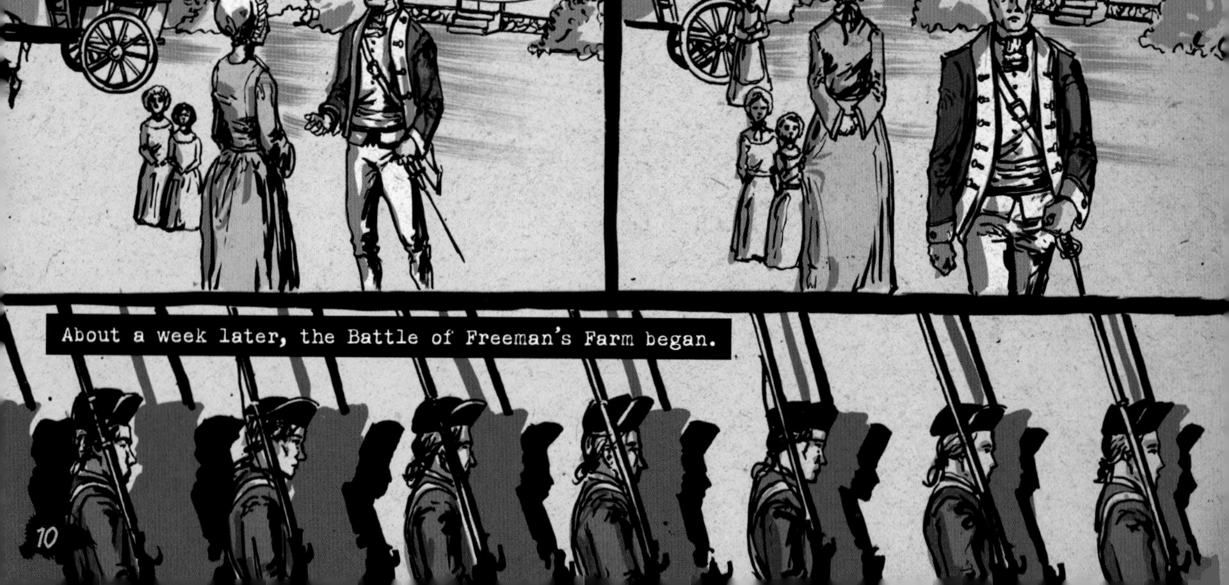
About a week later, the Battle of Freeman's Farm began.

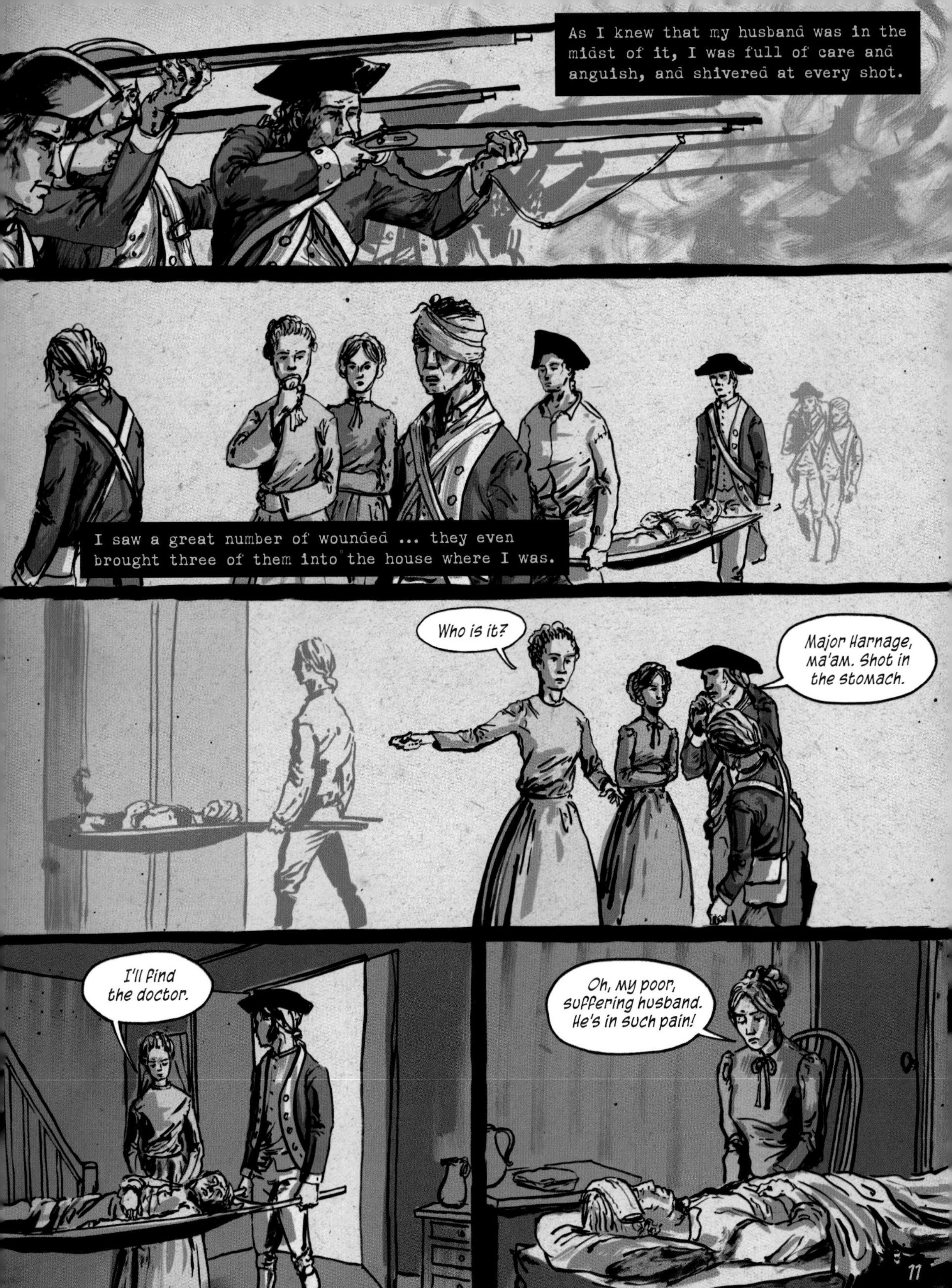

As I knew that my husband was in the midst of it, I was full of care and anguish, and shivered at every shot.
I saw a great number of wounded ... they even brought three of them into the house where I was.
Who is it?
Major Harnage, ma'am. Shot in the stomach.
I'll find the doctor.
Oh, my poor, suffering husband. He's in such pain!

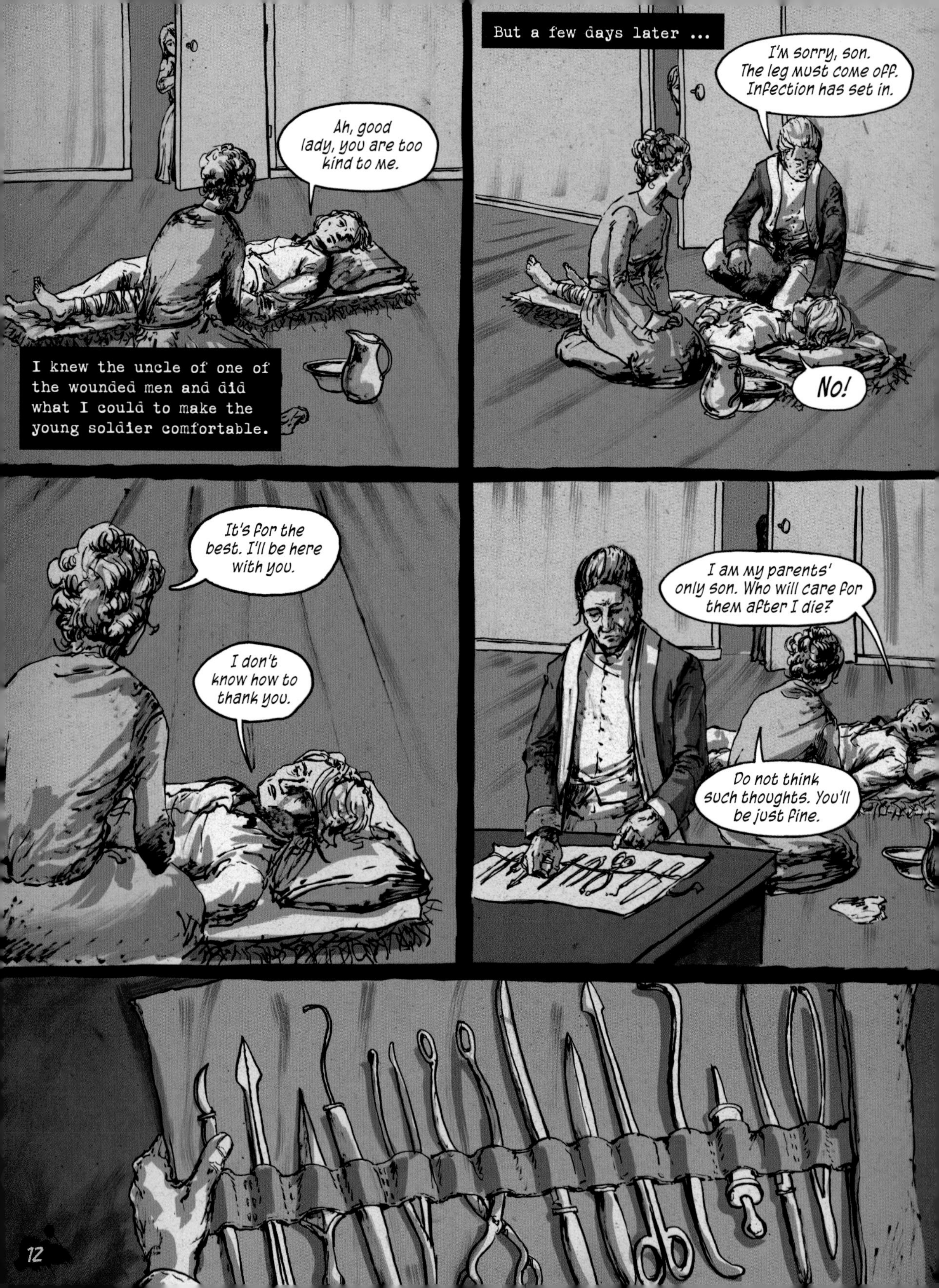
Ah, good lady, you are too kind to me.
I knew the uncle of one of the wounded men and did what I could to make the young soldier comfortable.
But a few days later ...
I'm sorry, son. The leg must come off. Infection has set in.
No!
It's for the best. I'll be here with you.
I don't know how to thank you.
I am my parents' only son. Who will care for them after I die?
Do not think such thoughts. You'll be just fine.

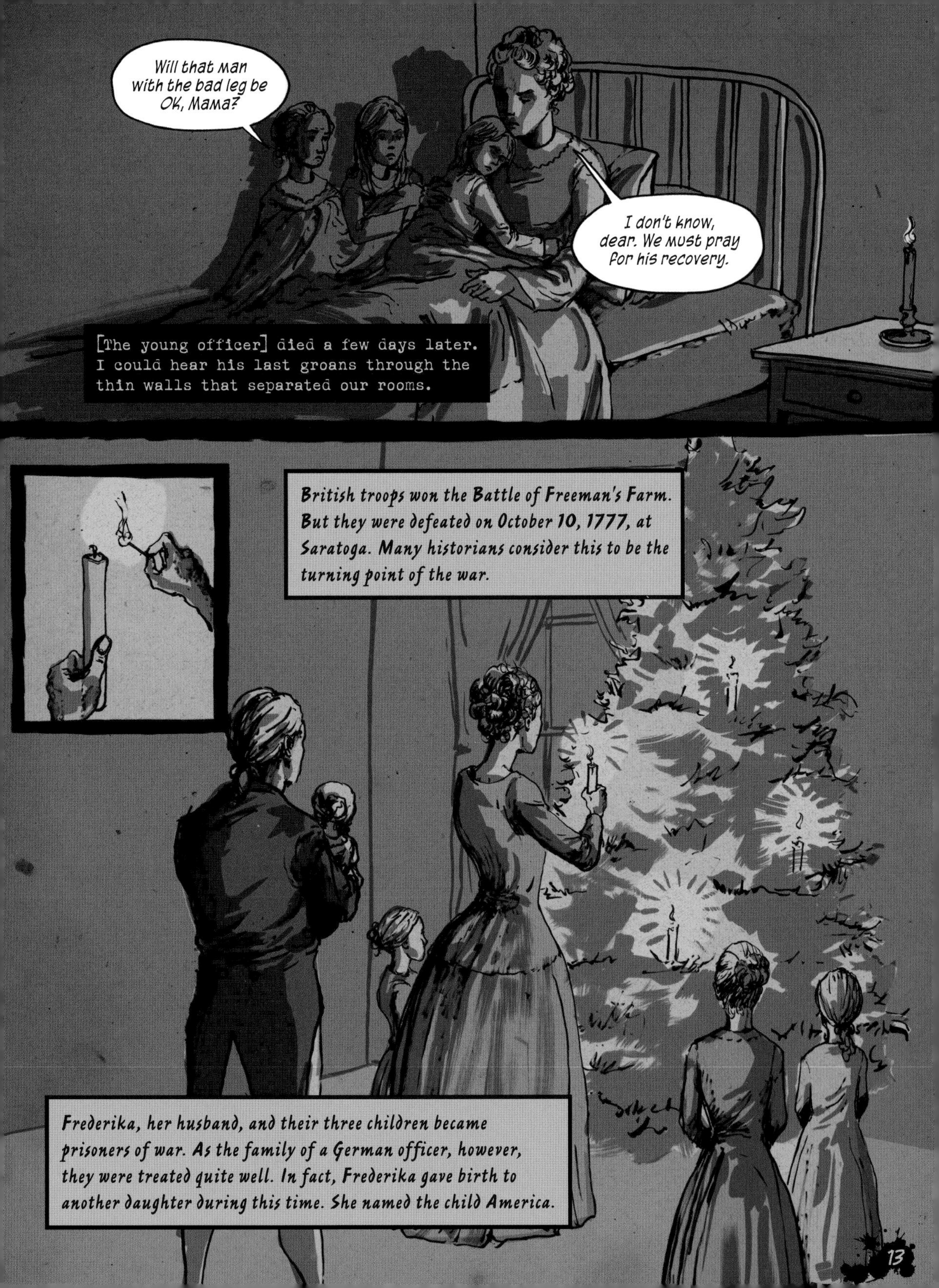
Will that man with the bad leg be OK, Mama?
I don't know, dear. We must pray for his recovery.
[The young officer] died a few days later. I could hear his last groans through the thin walls that separated our rooms.
British troops won the Battle of Freeman's Farm. But they were defeated on October 10, 1777, at Saratoga. Many historians consider this to be the turning point of the war.
Frederika, her husband, and their three children became prisoners of war. As the family of a German officer, however, they were treated quite well. In fact, Frederika gave birth to another daughter during this time. She named the child America.

CH. 4

Lydia Darragh: Spying in Philadelphia

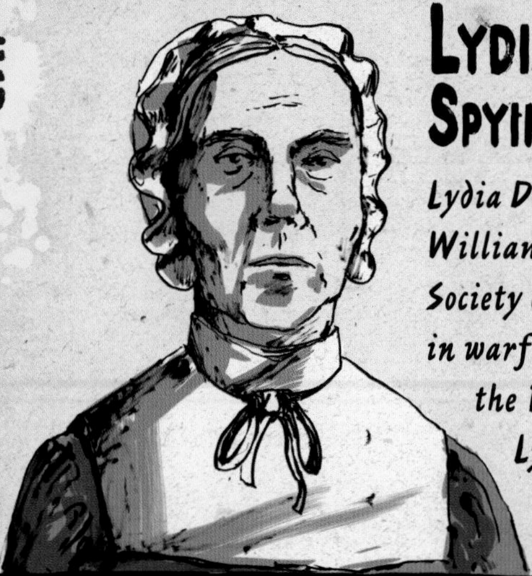

Lydia Darragh lived in Philadelphia with her husband, William. They belonged to a religious group called the Society of Friends, or Quakers. Quakers did not believe in warfare, and most Quakers remained neutral during the Revolutionary War. They didn't take sides. Lydia, however, favored independence. She kept her feelings secret.

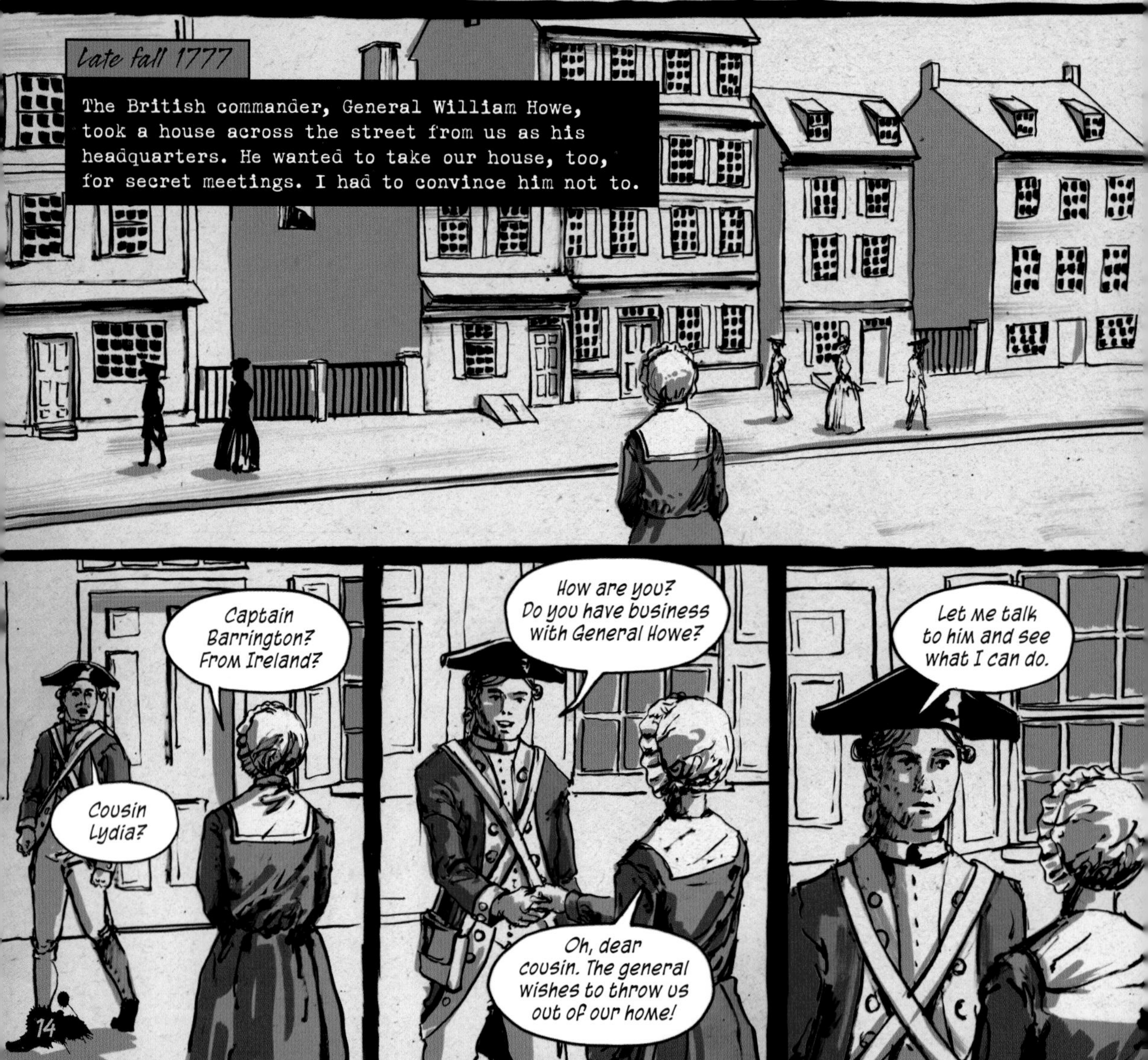
Late fall 1777
The British commander, General William Howe, took a house across the street from us as his headquarters. He wanted to take our house, too, for secret meetings. I had to convince him not to.
Captain Barrington? From Ireland?
Cousin Lydia?
How are you? Do you have business with General Howe?
Oh, dear cousin. The general wishes to throw us out of our home!
Let me talk to him and see what I can do.

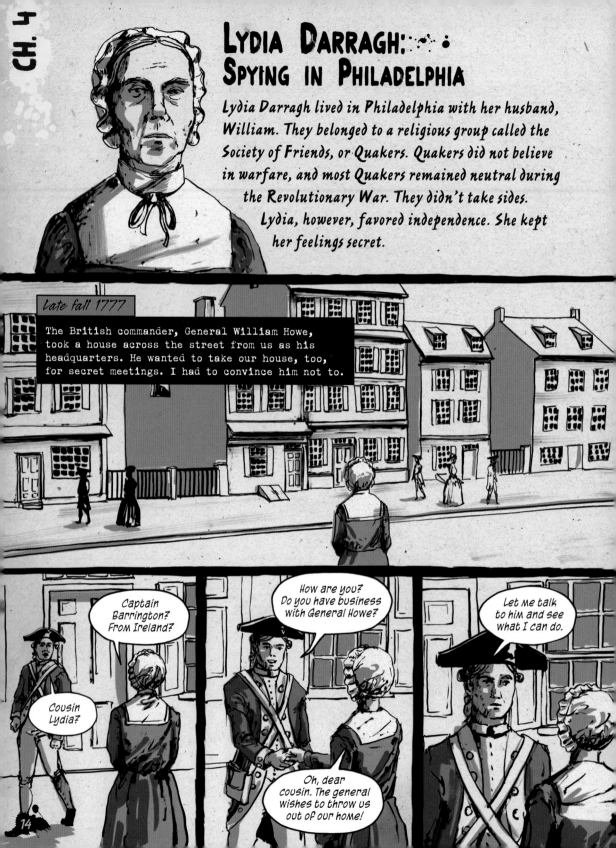

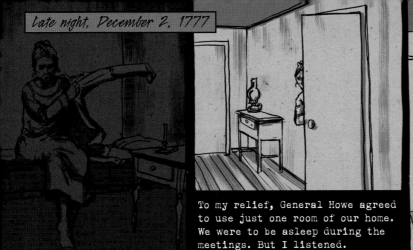

To my relief, General Howe agreed to use just one room of our home. We were to be asleep during the meetings. But I listened.

On December 4, we attack Washington's troops here, at White Marsh. We'll take them by surprise.

My eldest son had broken with Quaker tradition and joined the Continental Army.

He was now in harm's way. I knew spying was dangerous, but I had to protect my family.

They'll never know what hit them.

I listened as long as I could. Then I rushed to my room and pretended to sleep.

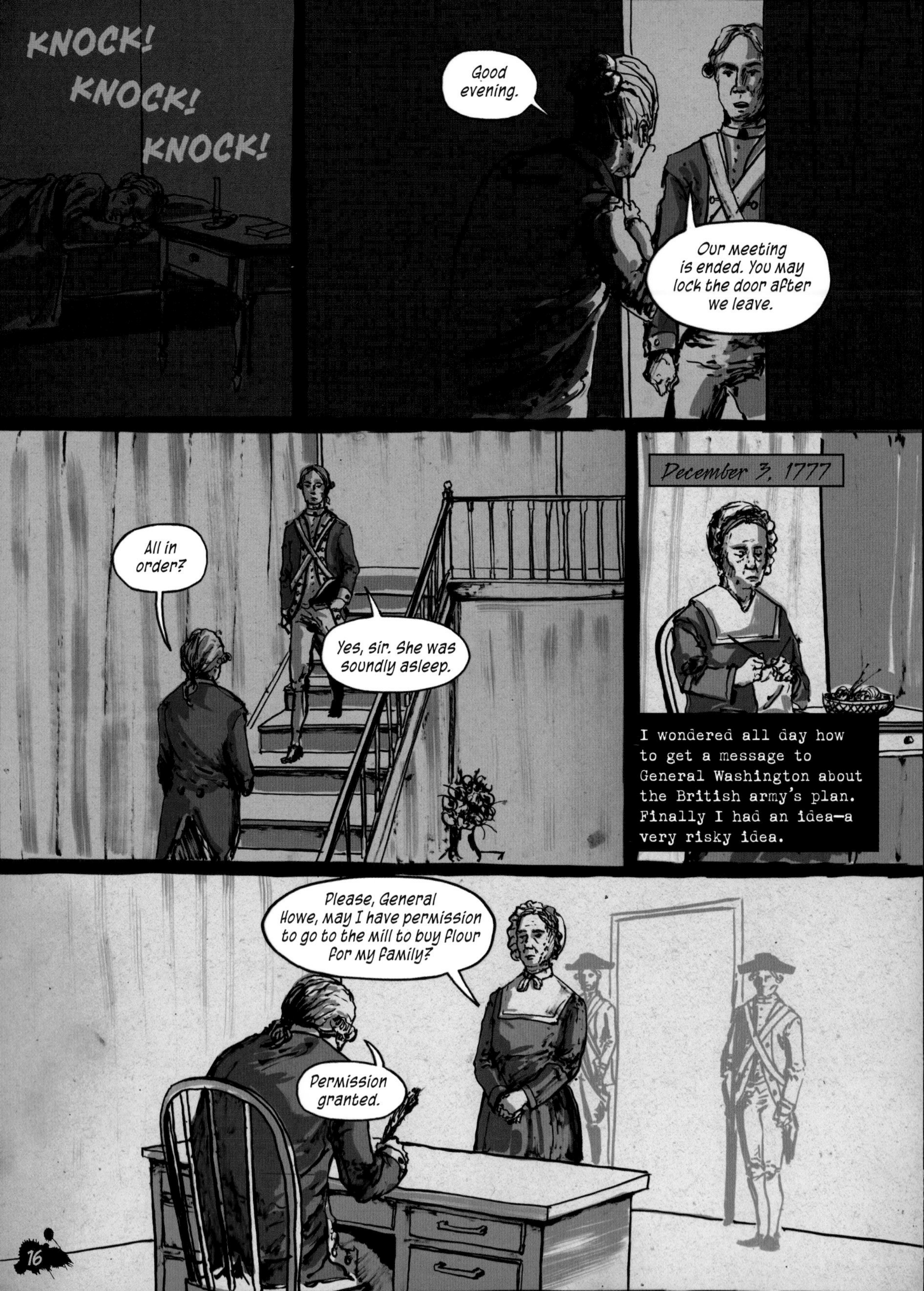
KNOCK!
KNOCK!
KNOCK!
Good evening.
Our meeting is ended. You may lock the door after we leave.
All in order?
Yes, sir. She was soundly asleep.
December 3, 1777
I wondered all day how to get a message to General Washington about the British army's plan. Finally I had an idea—a very risky idea.
Please, General Howe, may I have permission to go to the mill to buy flour for my family?
Permission granted.

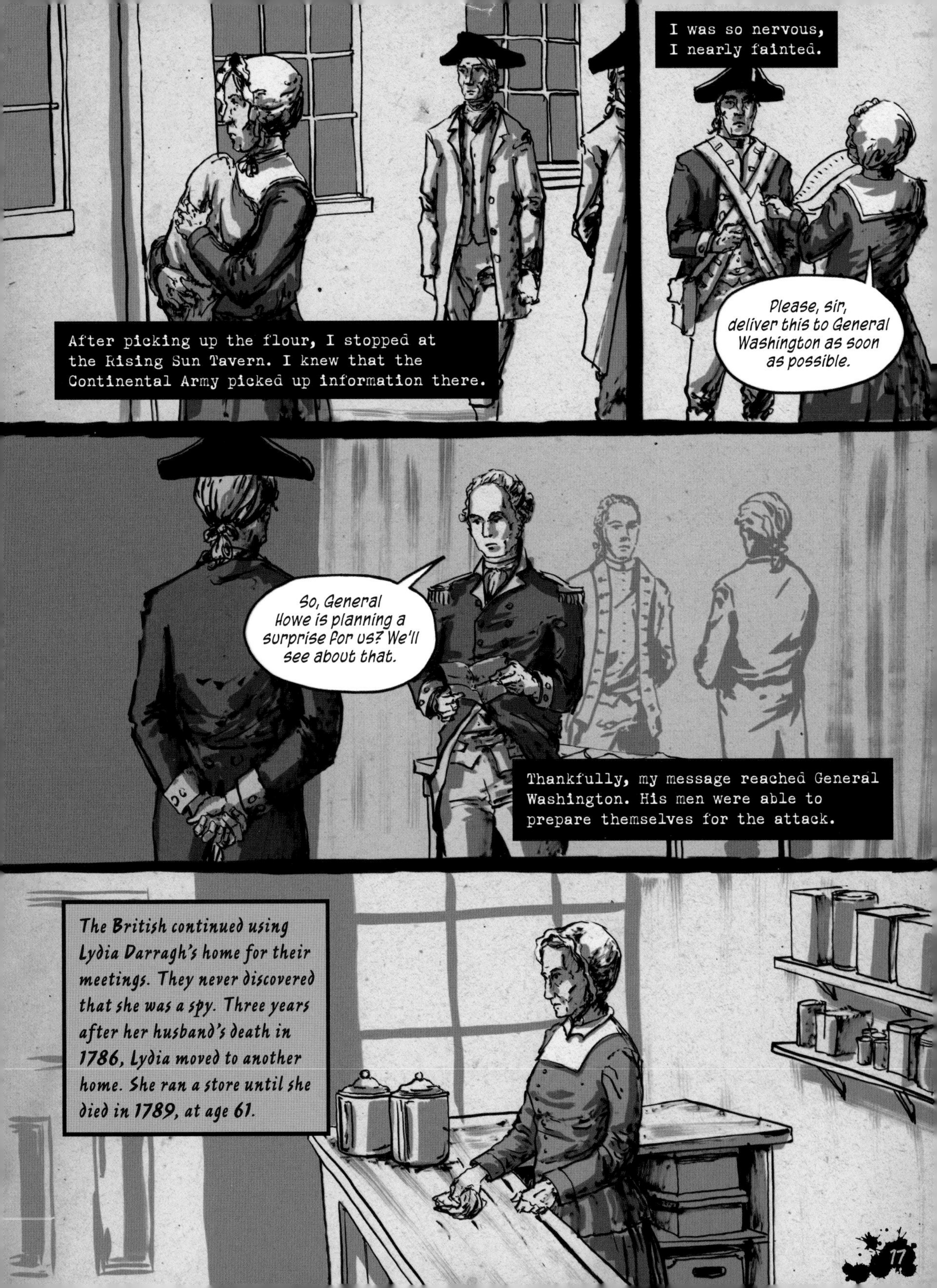
After picking up the flour, I stopped at the Rising Sun Tavern. I knew that the Continental Army picked up information there.
I was so nervous, I nearly fainted.
Please, sir, deliver this to General Washington as soon as possible.
So, General Howe is planning a surprise for us? We'll see about that.
Thankfully, my message reached General Washington. His men were able to prepare themselves for the attack.
The British continued using Lydia Darragh's home for their meetings. They never discovered that she was a spy. Three years after her husband's death in 1786, Lydia moved to another home. She ran a store until she died in 1789, at age 61.

CH. 5

Albigence Waldo: The Battle of White Marsh

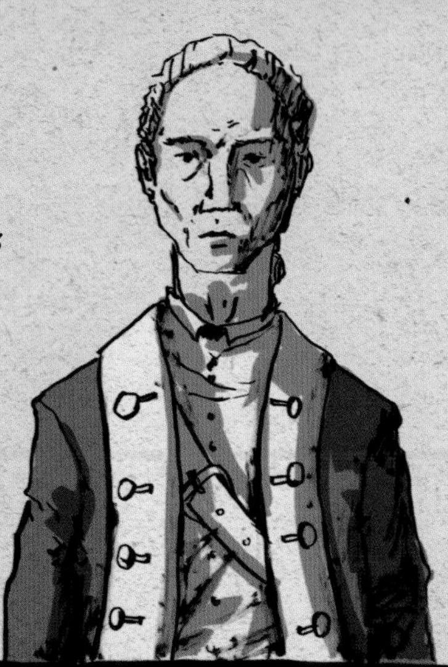

On July 6, 1775, Albigence Waldo became a surgeon's mate in a Connecticut regiment. Like most doctors of the time, he had learned medicine by studying with another doctor. In September 1777 Waldo's regiment joined General George Washington at White Marsh, about 13 miles (21 kilometers) northwest of Philadelphia, Pennsylvania.

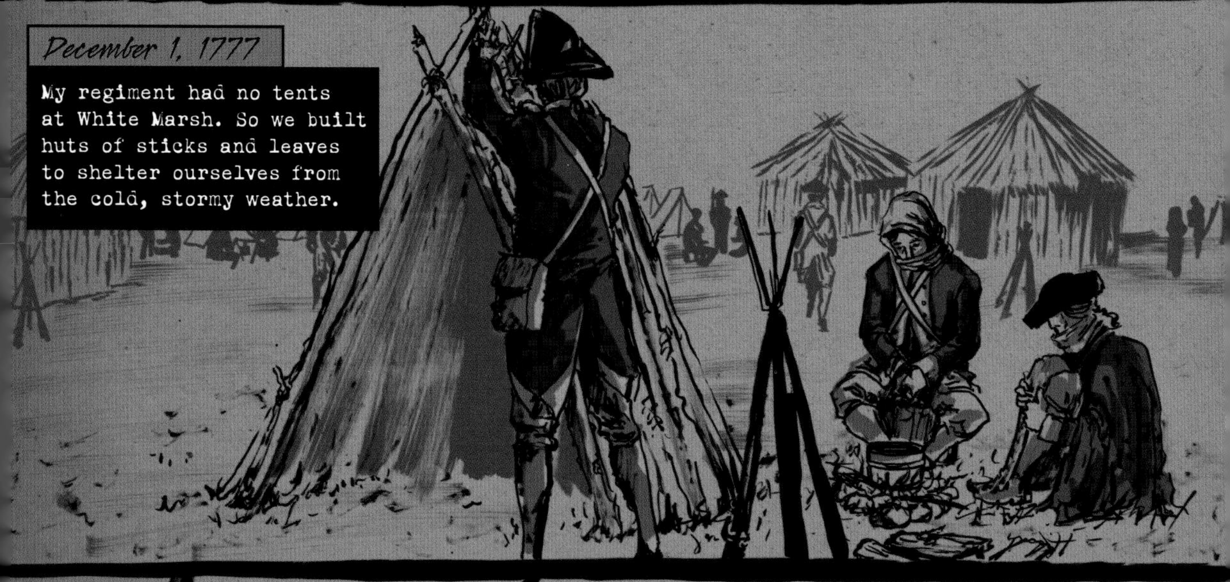
December 1, 1777
My regiment had no tents at White Marsh. So we built huts of sticks and leaves to shelter ourselves from the cold, stormy weather.

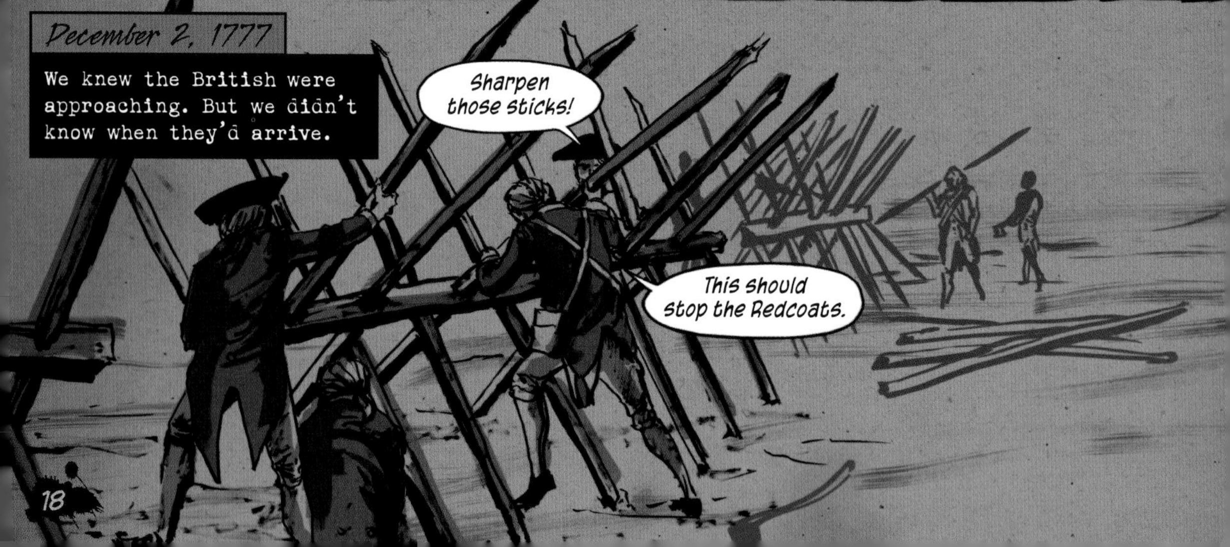
December 2, 1777
We knew the British were approaching. But we didn't know when they'd arrive.
Sharpen those sticks!
This should stop the Redcoats.

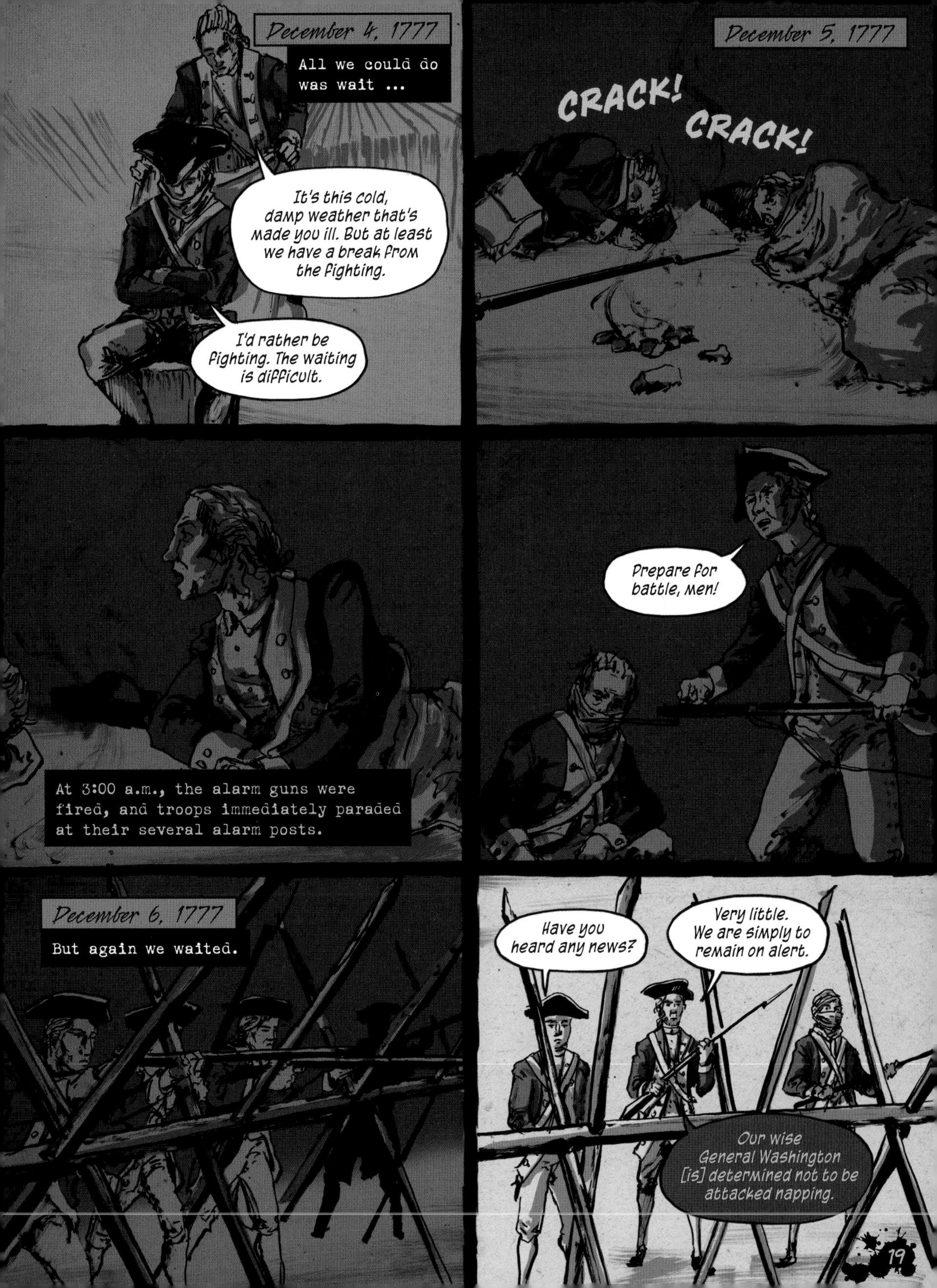
December 4, 1777
All we could do was wait ...
It's this cold, damp weather that's made you ill. But at least we have a break from the fighting.
I'd rather be fighting. The waiting is difficult.
December 5, 1777
CRACK! CRACK!
At 3:00 a.m., the alarm guns were fired, and troops immediately paraded at their several alarm posts.
Prepare for battle, men!
December 6, 1777
But again we waited.
Have you heard any news?
Very little. We are simply to remain on alert.
Our wise General Washington [is] determined not to be attacked napping.

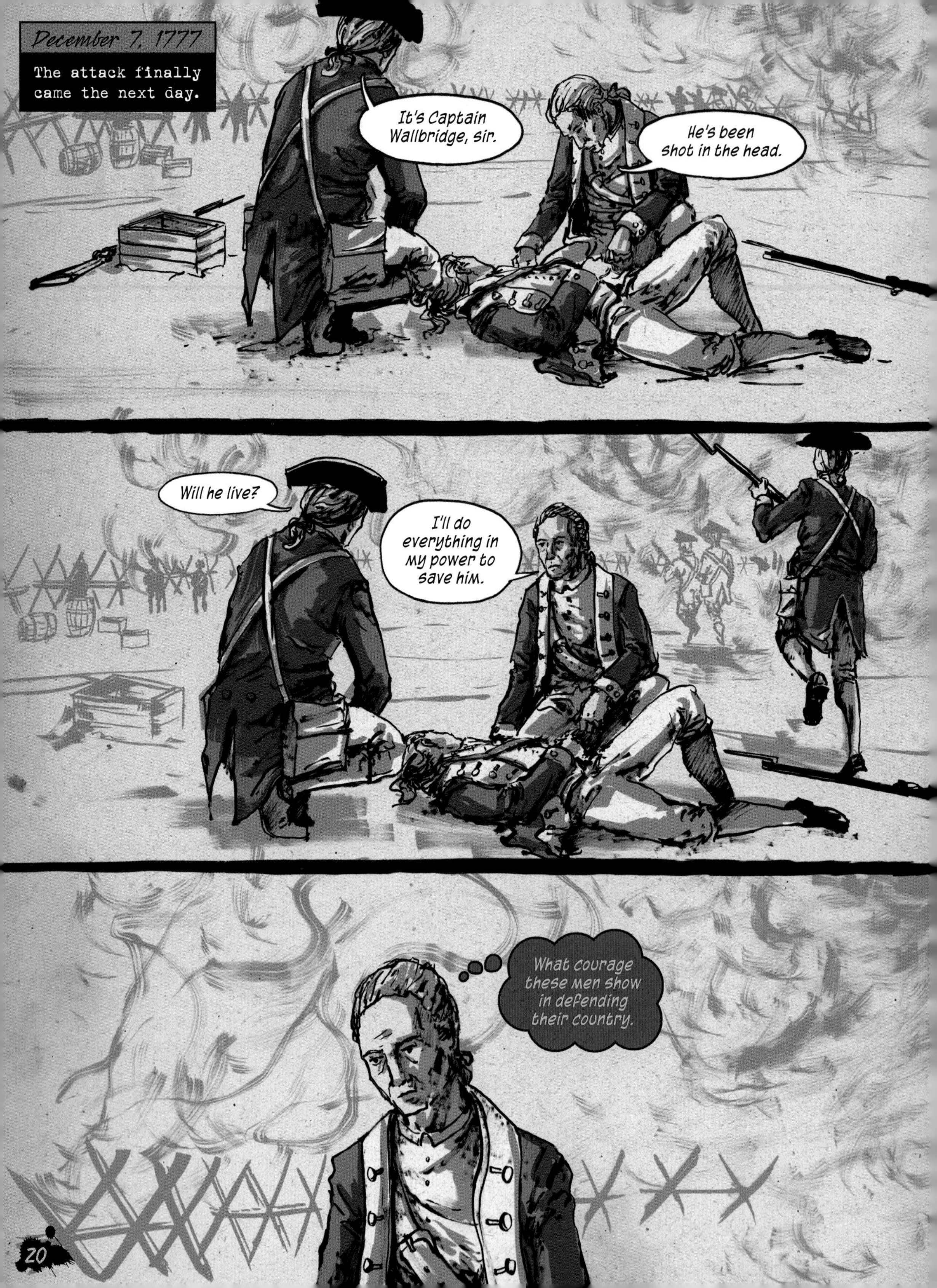
December 7, 1777
The attack finally came the next day.
It's Captain Wallbridge, sir.
He's been shot in the head.
Will he live?
I'll do everything in my power to save him.
What courage these men show in defending their country.

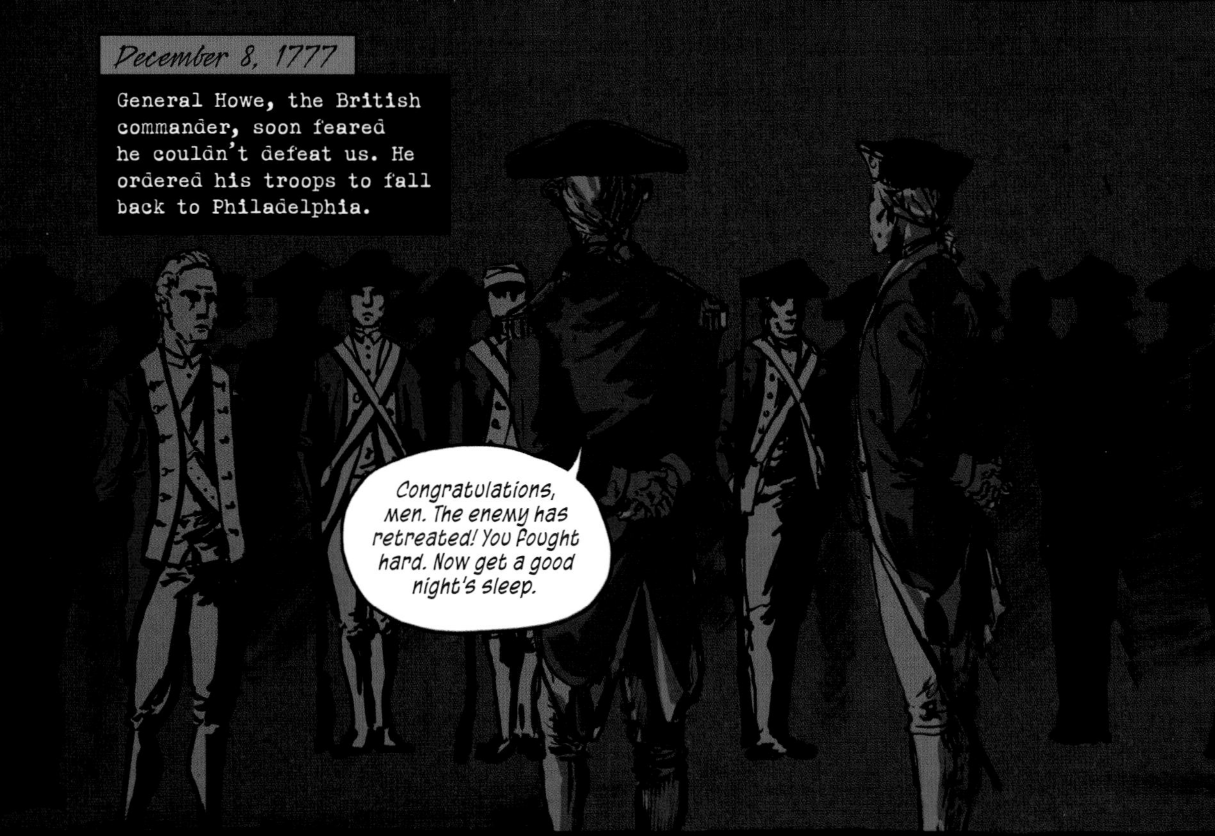
December 8, 1777
General Howe, the British commander, soon feared he couldn't defeat us. He ordered his troops to fall back to Philadelphia.
Congratulations, men. The enemy has retreated! You fought hard. Now get a good night's sleep.

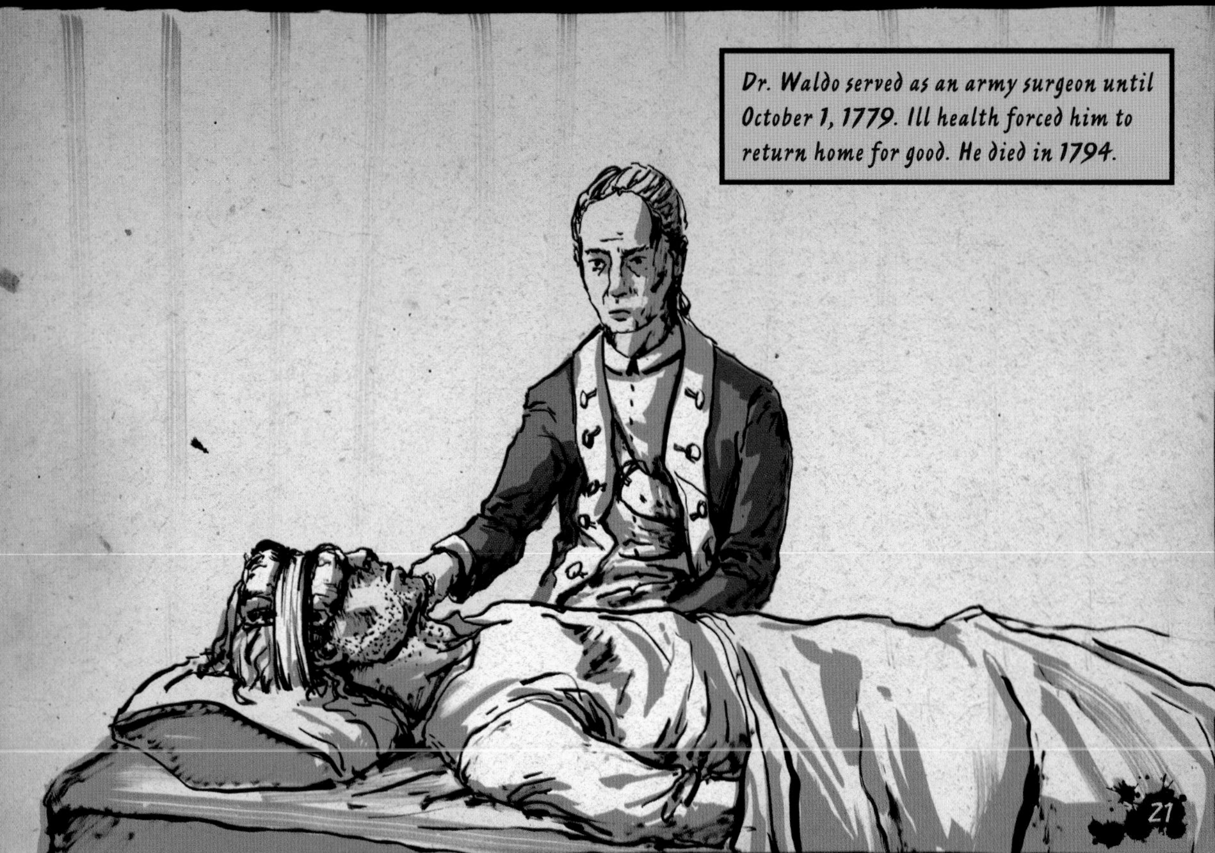
Dr. Waldo served as an army surgeon until October 1, 1779. Ill health forced him to return home for good. He died in 1794.

CH. 6 Lieutenant Anthony Allaire: The Battle of Monck's Corner

Anthony Allaire was a lieutenant in the Loyal American Volunteers. This company remained loyal to King George III and fought with the British against George Washington's forces. Allaire became the assistant to British colonel Patrick Ferguson, and went with him to South Carolina to fight the rebels.

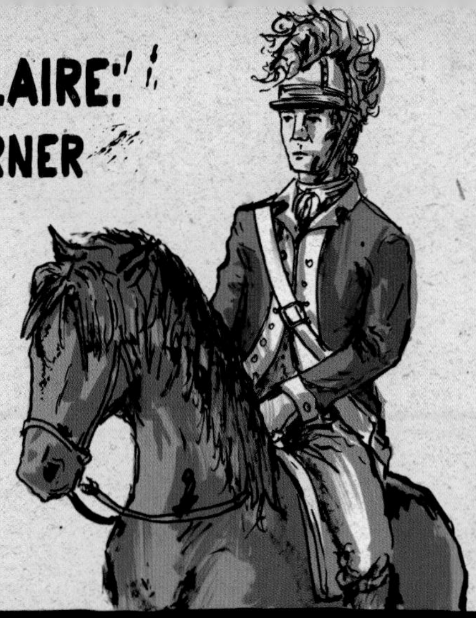

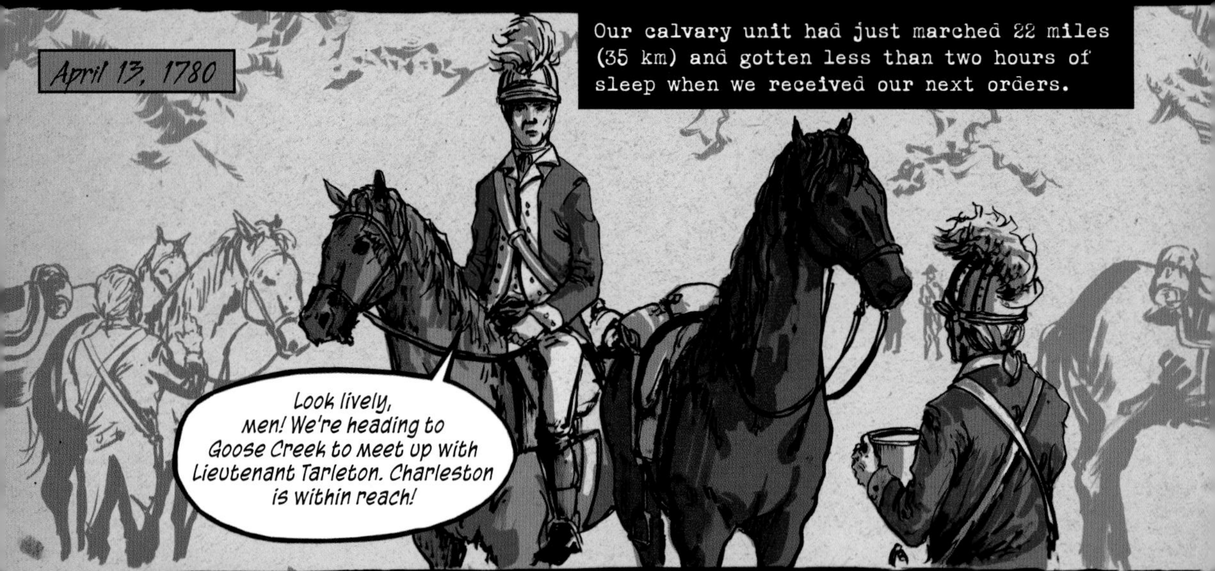

April 13, 1780
Our calvary unit had just marched 22 miles (35 km) and gotten less than two hours of sleep when we received our next orders.
Look lively, men! We're heading to Goose Creek to meet up with Lieutenant Tarleton. Charleston is within reach!

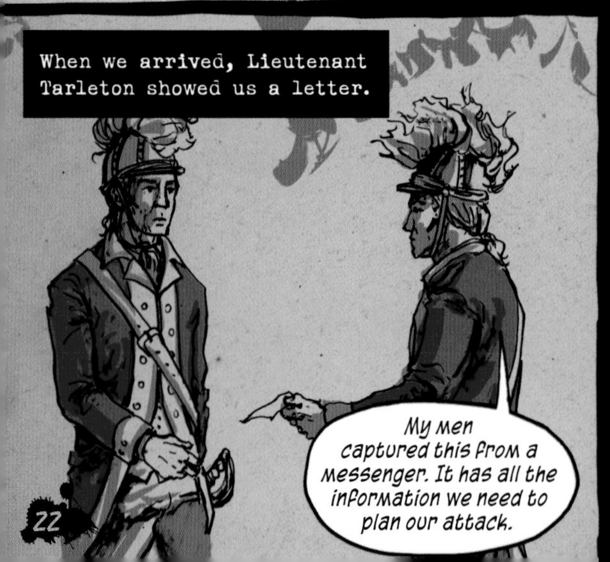

When we arrived, Lieutenant Tarleton showed us a letter.
My men captured this from a messenger. It has all the information we need to plan our attack.

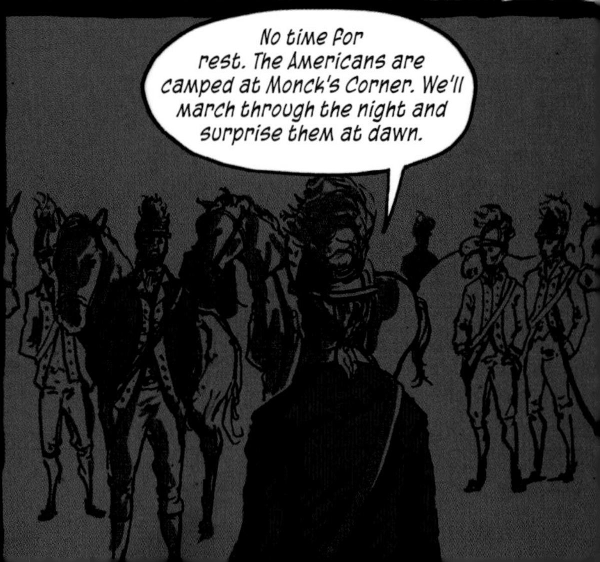

No time for rest. The Americans are camped at Monck's Corner. We'll march through the night and surprise them at dawn.

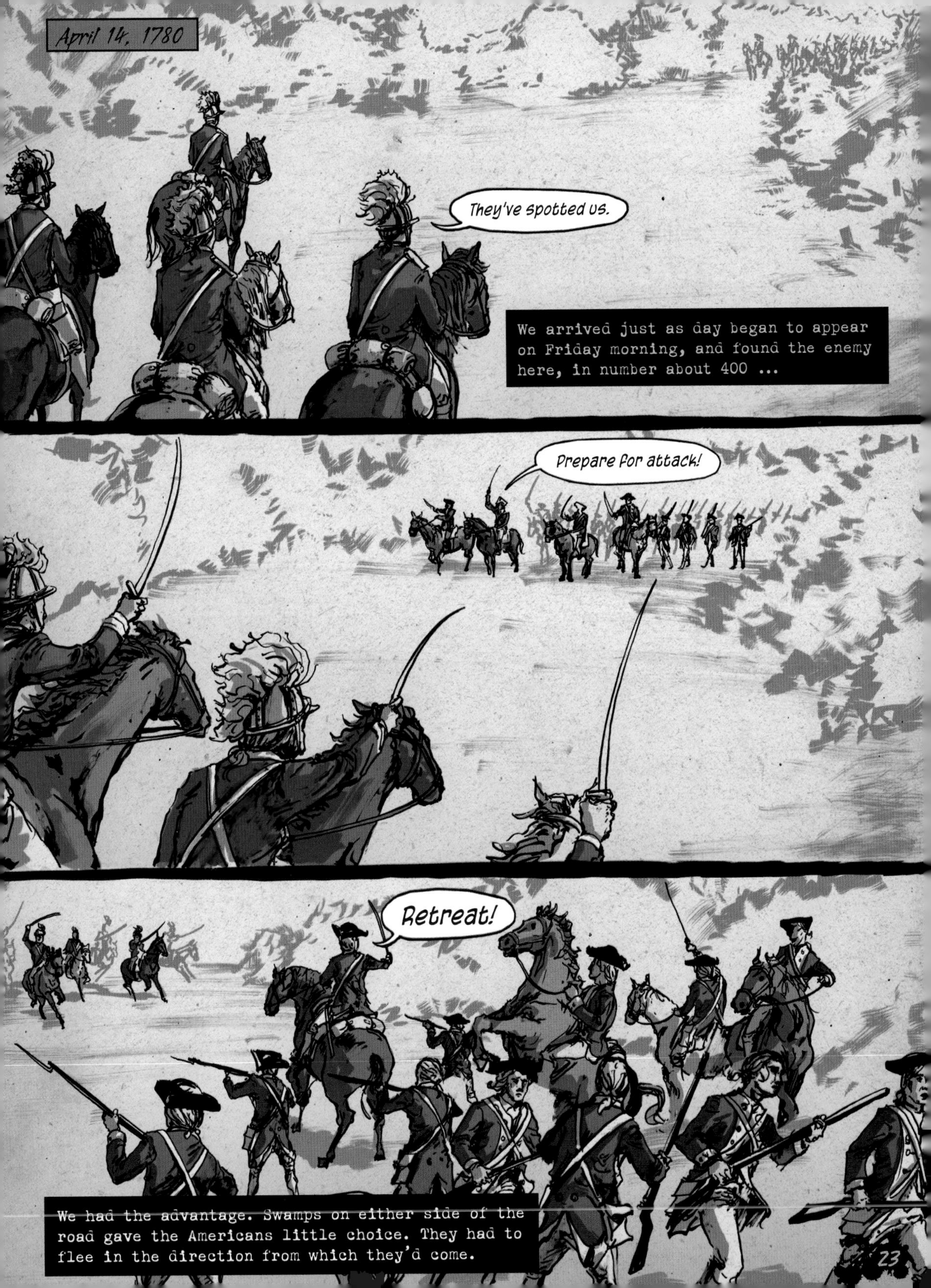

April 14, 1780
They've spotted us.
We arrived just as day began to appear on Friday morning, and found the enemy here, in number about 400 ...
Prepare for attack!
Retreat!
We had the advantage. Swamps on either side of the road gave the Americans little choice. They had to flee in the direction from which they'd come.

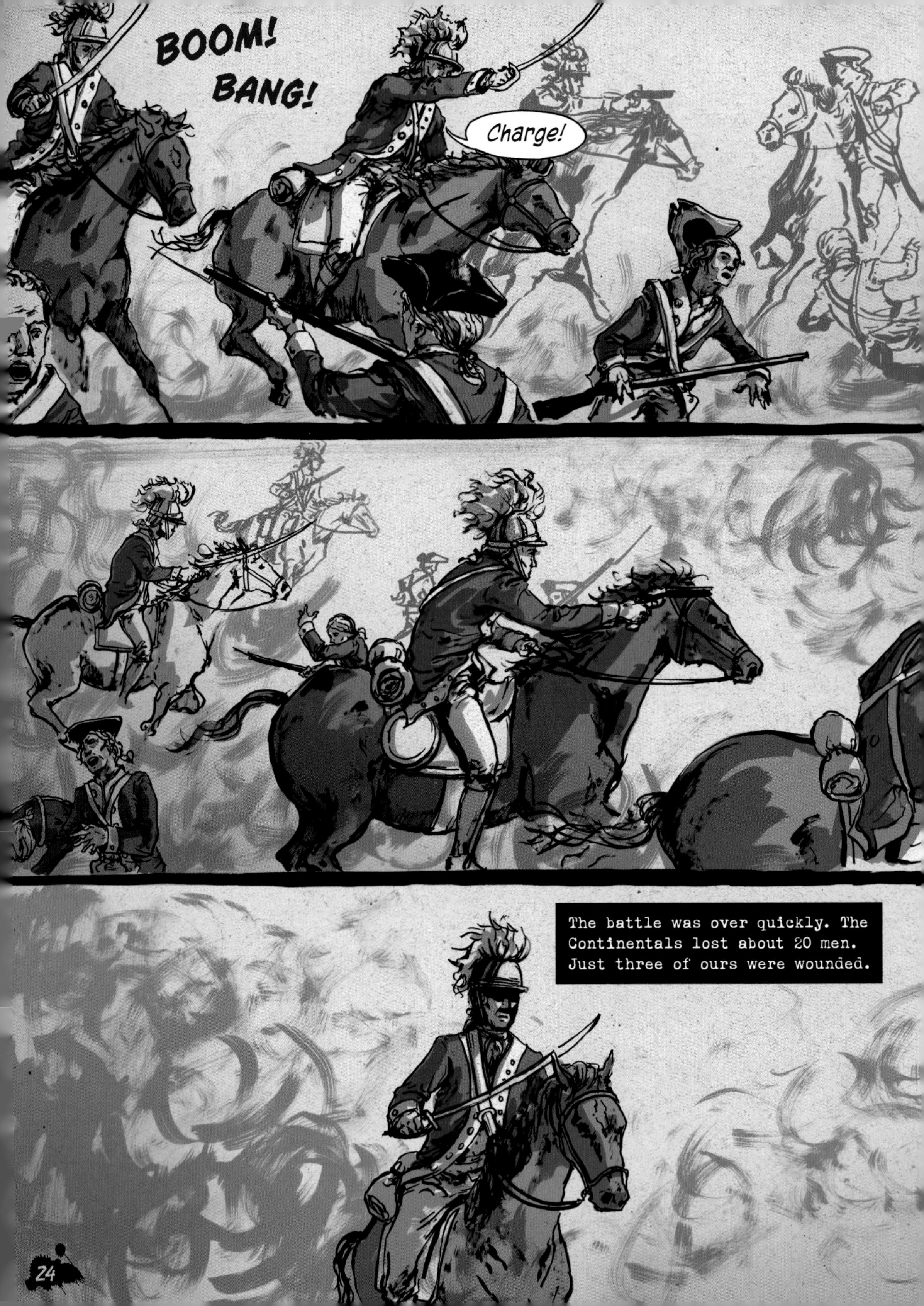
BOOM!
BANG!
Charge!
The battle was over quickly. The Continentals lost about 20 men. Just three of ours were wounded.

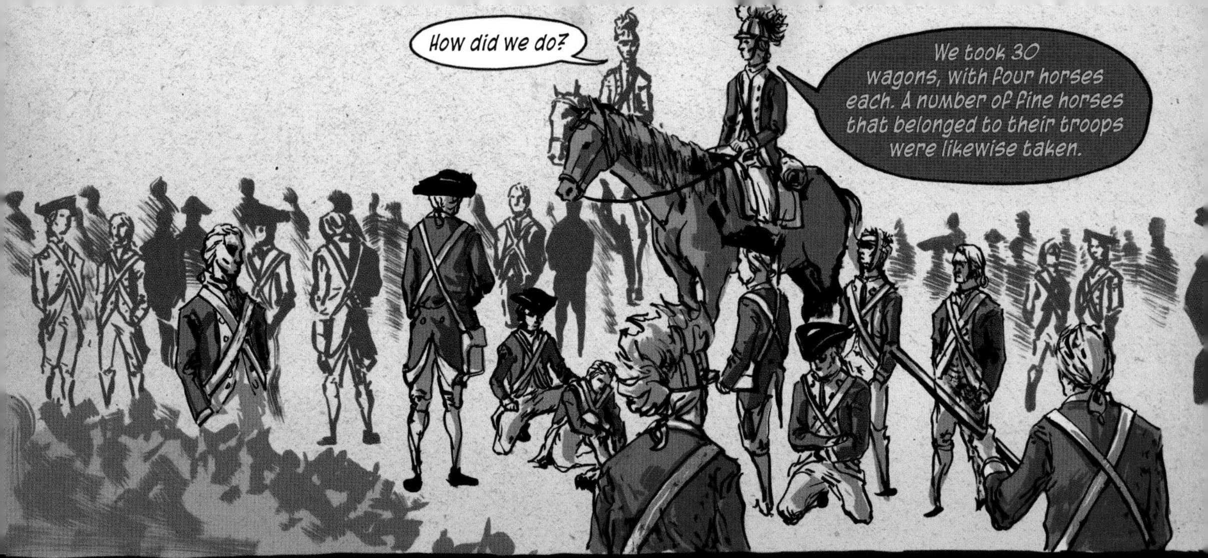
How did we do?
We took 30 wagons, with four horses each. A number of fine horses that belonged to their troops were likewise taken.

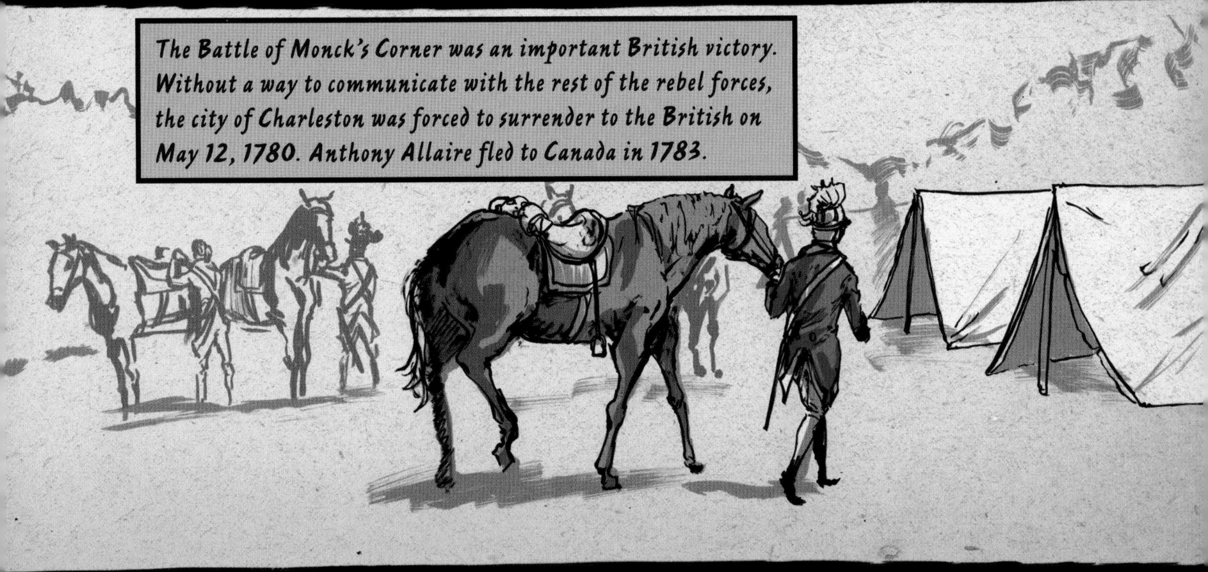
The Battle of Monck's Corner was an important British victory. Without a way to communicate with the rest of the rebel forces, the city of Charleston was forced to surrender to the British on May 12, 1780. Anthony Allaire fled to Canada in 1783.

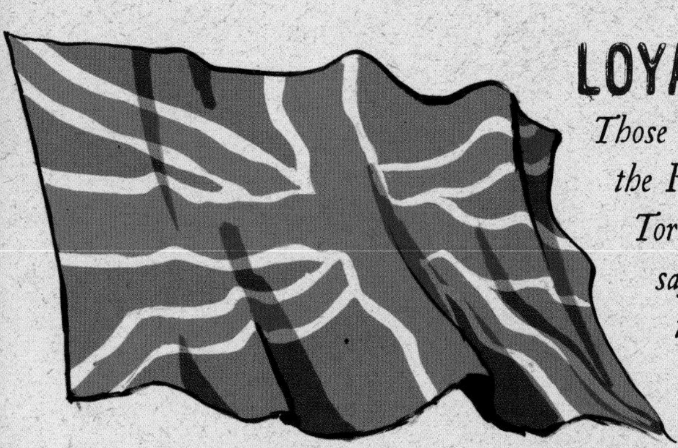

LOYALISTS

Those who remained loyal to Great Britain during the Revolutionary War were called Loyalists, Tories, or King's Men. They felt the colonies were safer under British protection, and they wanted to continue trading with Great Britain. About one-fifth of the colonists were loyalists. After the war, many left for England. Others went to Canada or other British colonies.

CH. 7

SARAH OSBORN BENJAMIN: THE BATTLE OF YORKTOWN

Sarah Osborn Benjamin was a camp follower—a woman who followed her husband to war. She cooked, washed, and sewed for the soldiers in her husband's New York regiment. In September 1781 Sarah followed the Continental Army from West Point, New York, to Yorktown, Virginia. It would be her final taste of battle.

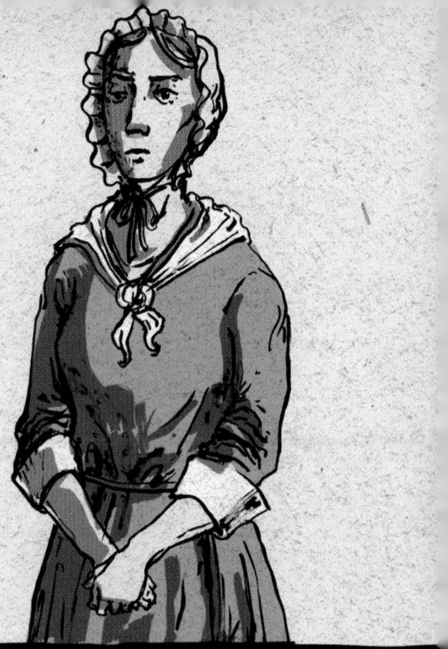

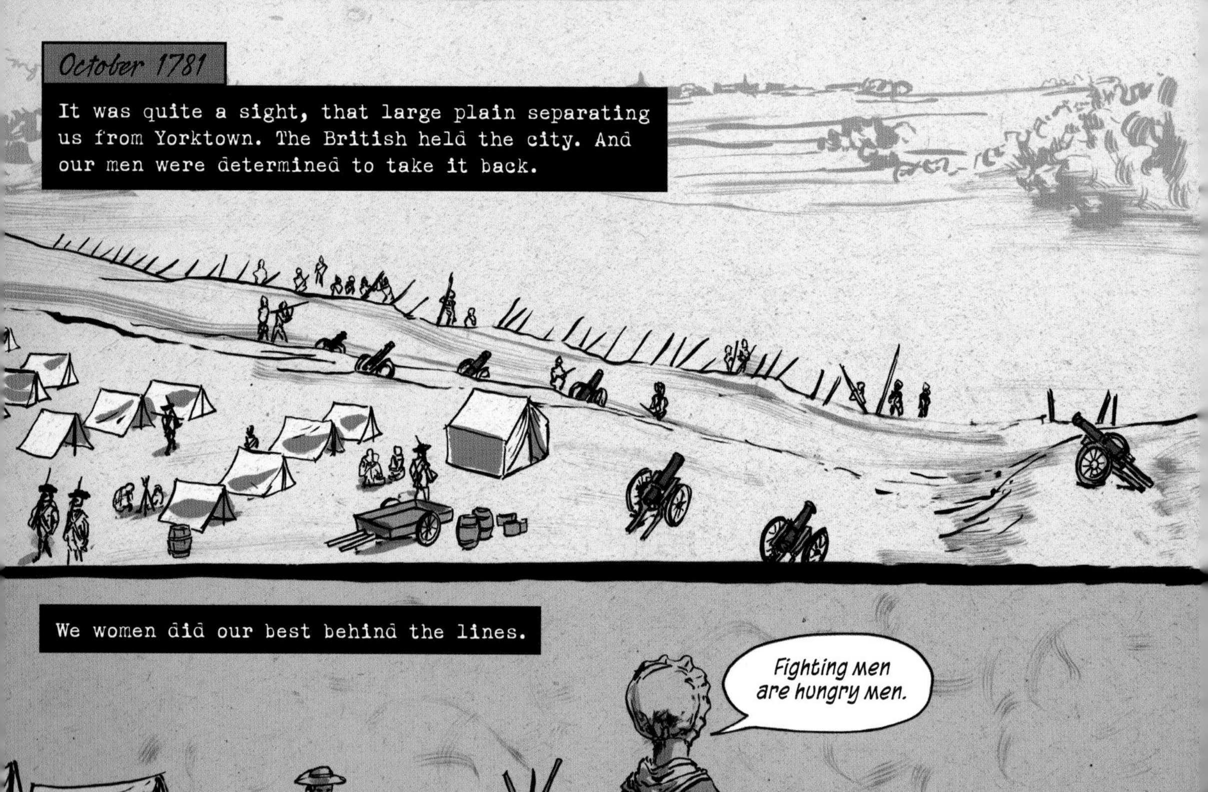
October 1781
It was quite a sight, that large plain separating us from Yorktown. The British held the city. And our men were determined to take it back.

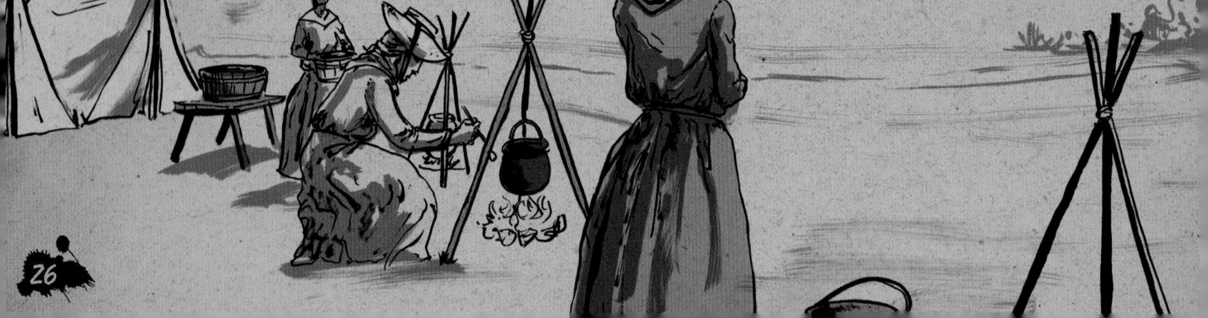
We women did our best behind the lines.
Fighting men are hungry men.

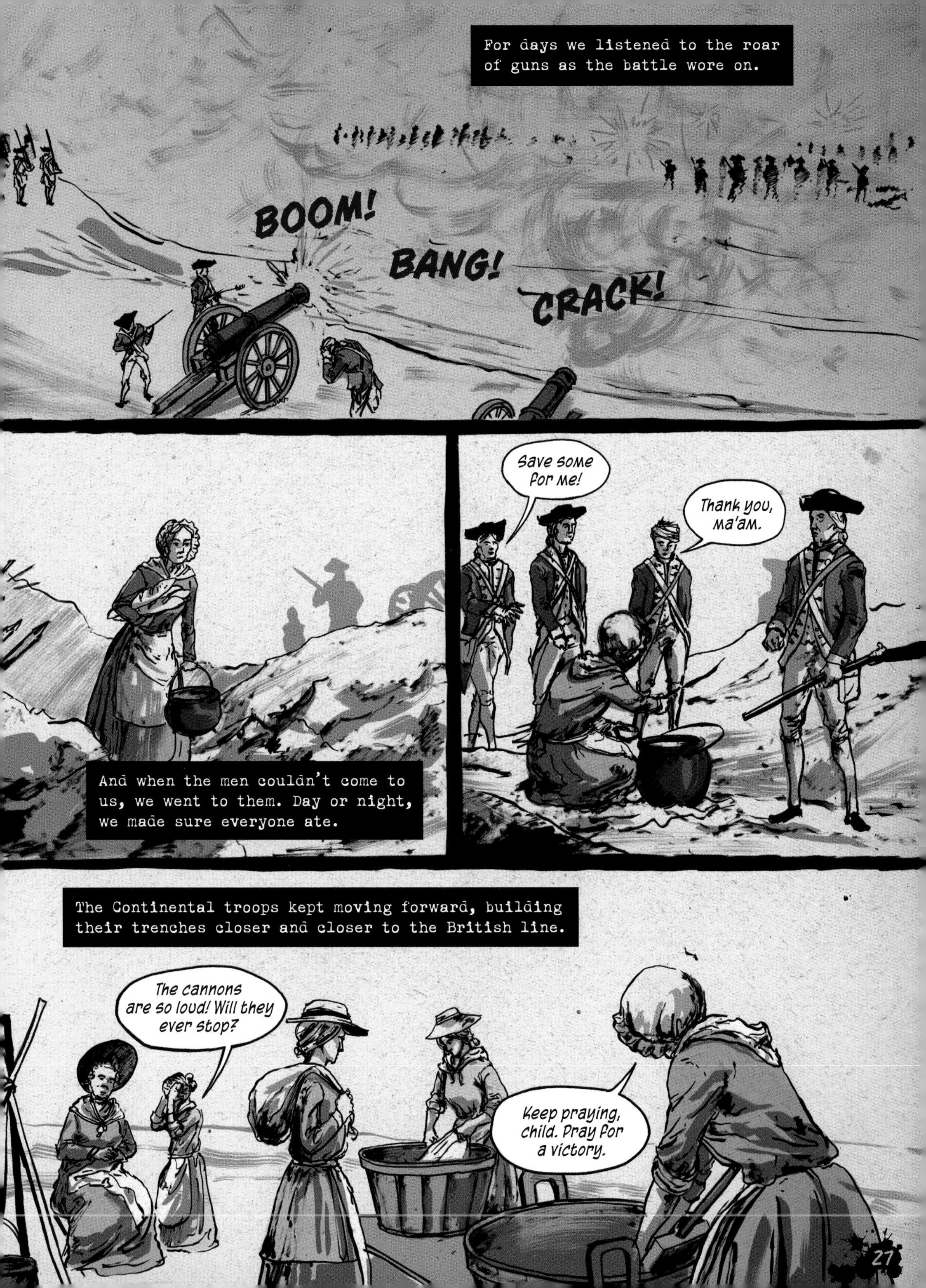

For days we listened to the roar of guns as the battle wore on.
BOOM!
BANG!
CRACK!
And when the men couldn't come to us, we went to them. Day or night, we made sure everyone ate.
Save some for me!
Thank you, ma'am.
The Continental troops kept moving forward, building their trenches closer and closer to the British line.
The cannons are so loud! Will they ever stop?
Keep praying, child. Pray for a victory.

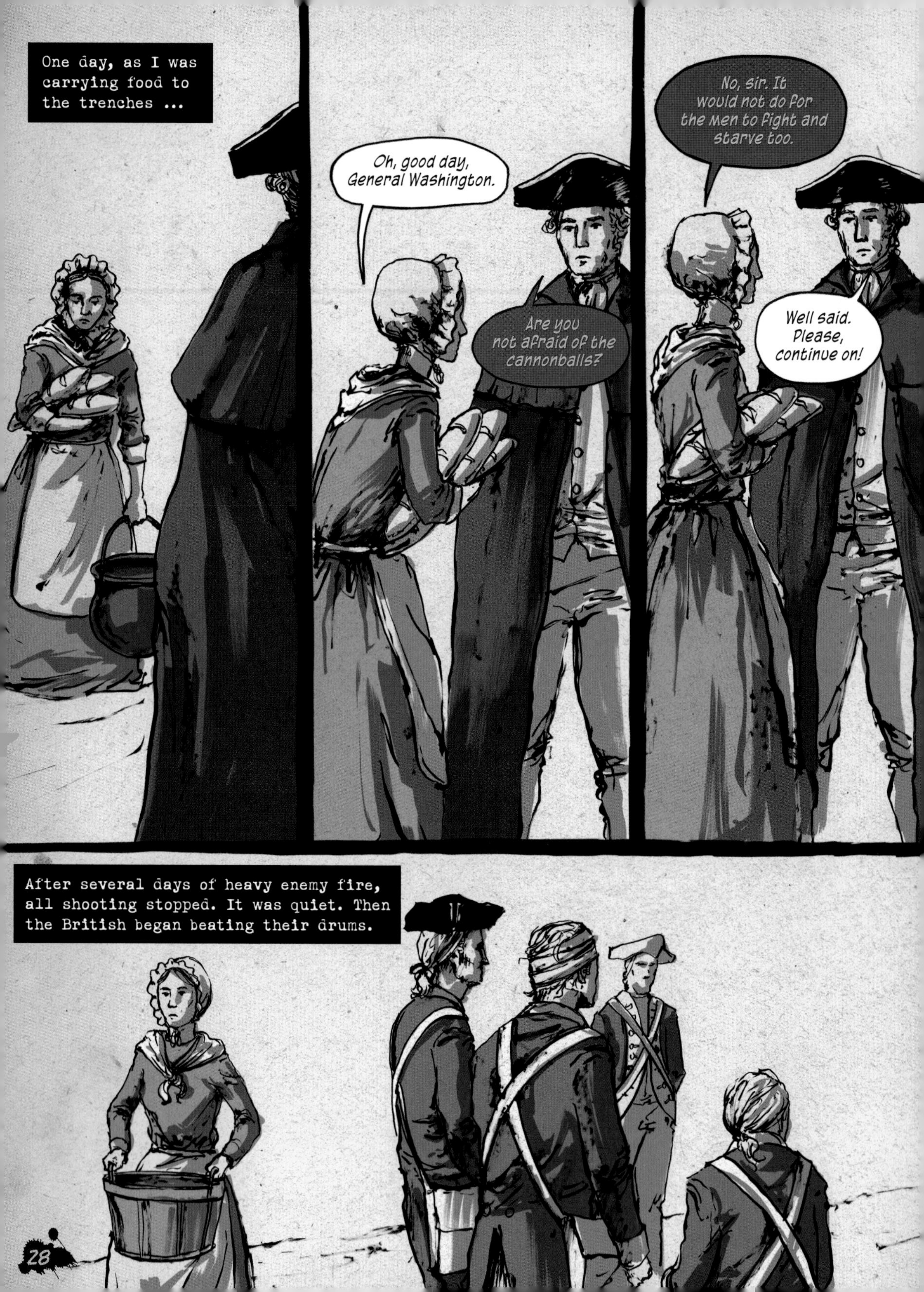
One day, as I was carrying food to the trenches ...
Oh, good day, General Washington.
Are you not afraid of the cannonballs?
No, sir. It would not do for the men to fight and starve too.
Well said. Please, continue on!
After several days of heavy enemy fire, all shooting stopped. It was quiet. Then the British began beating their drums.

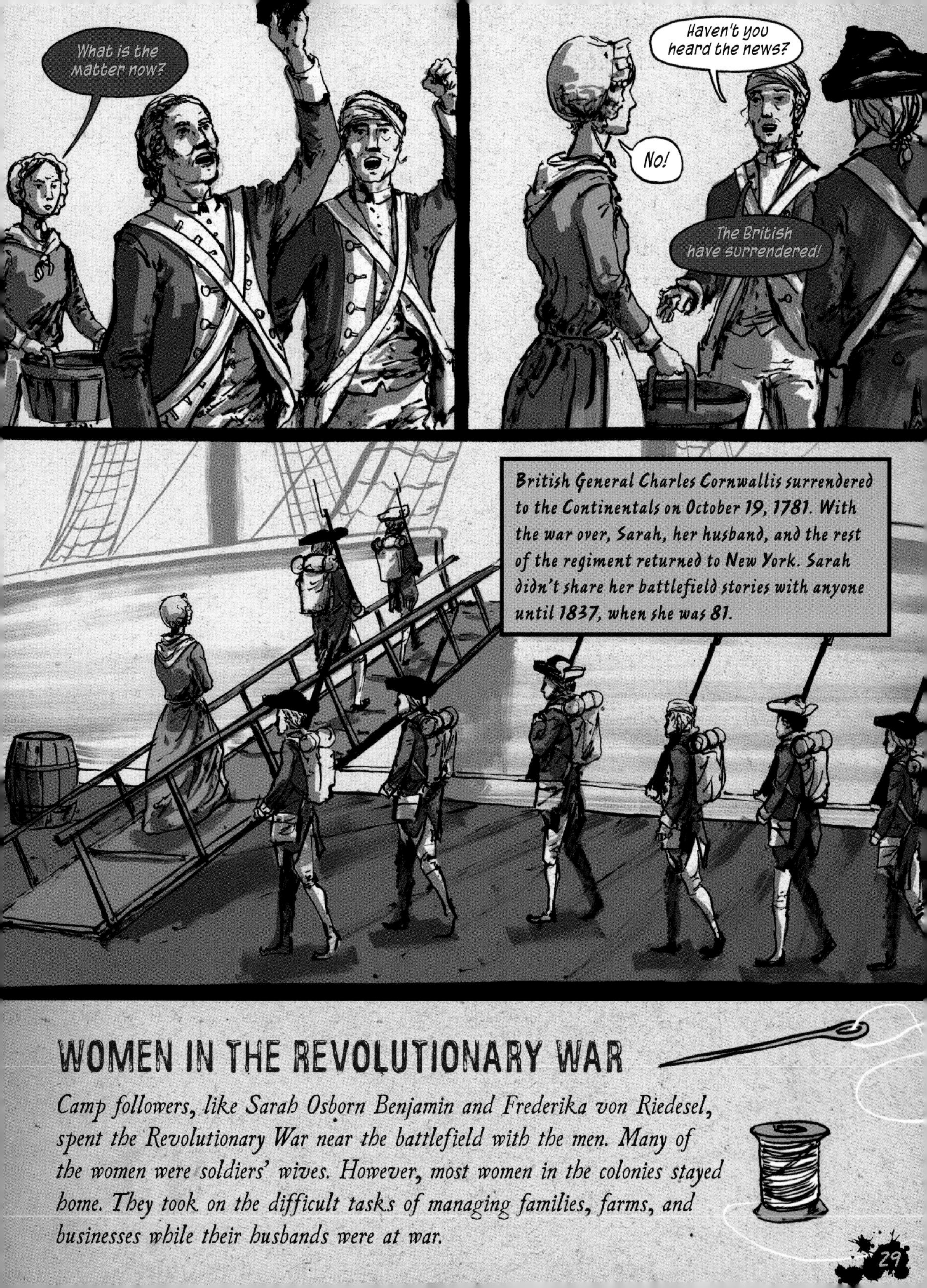
What is the matter now?
Haven't you heard the news?
No!
The British have surrendered!
British General Charles Cornwallis surrendered to the Continentals on October 19, 1781. With the war over, Sarah, her husband, and the rest of the regiment returned to New York. Sarah didn't share her battlefield stories with anyone until 1837, when she was 81.

WOMEN IN THE REVOLUTIONARY WAR

Camp followers, like Sarah Osborn Benjamin and Frederika von Riedesel, spent the Revolutionary War near the battlefield with the men. Many of the women were soldiers' wives. However, most women in the colonies stayed home. They took on the difficult tasks of managing families, farms, and businesses while their husbands were at war.

GLOSSARY

AMMUNITION (am-yuh-NI-shuhn)—bullets and other objects that can be fired from weapons

CAVALRY (KA-vuhl-ree)—soldiers who travel and fight on horseback

COLONY (KAH-luh-nee)—an area that has been settled by people from another country; a colony is ruled by another country

CONGRESS (KAHNG-gruhss)—a group of people who make laws

CONTINENTAL ARMY (kahn-tuh-NEN-tuhl AR-mee)—a military force made up of American colonists, led by George Washington

DECLARE (di-KLAYR)—to say something

LOYALIST (LOI-uh-list)—a colonist who was true to Great Britain during the Revolutionary War

PATRIOT (PAY-tree-uht)—a person who sided with the colonies during the Revolutionary War

REBEL (REB-uhl)—someone who fights against a government or ruler

REGIMENT (REJ-uh-muhnt)—a large group of soldiers who fight together as a unit

RETREAT (ri-TREET)—to move back or withdraw from a difficult situation

REVOLUTION (rev-uh-LOO-shun)—an uprising by a group of people against a system of government or a way of life

SURRENDER (suh-REN-dur)—to give up or admit defeat

TRENCH (TRENCH)—a long, deep area dug into the ground with dirt piled up on one side for defense

READ MORE

Doeden, Matt. *Weapons of the Revolutionary War*. Weapons of War. Mankato, Minn.: Capstone Press, 2009.

Kostyal, K.M., with the Colonial Williamsburg Foundation. *1776: A New Look at Revolutionary Williamsburg*. Washington, D.C.: National Geographic, 2009.

Murphy, Jim. *The Crossing: How George Washington Saved the American Revolution*. New York: Scholastic Press, 2010.

Raum, Elizabeth. *The Revolutionary War: An Interactive History Adventure*. You Choose Books. Mankato, Minn.: Capstone Press, 2010.

INTERNET SITES

FactHound offers a safe, fun way to find Internet sites related to this book. All sites on FactHound have been researched by our staff.

Here's all you do:

Visit www.facthound.com

Type in this code: 9781429686747

Super-cool stuff!

Check out projects, games and lots more at
www.capstonekids.com

INDEX

Allaire, Anthony, 22-25

Bangs, Isaac, 6-9
Battle of
   Bunker Hill, 5
   Freeman's Farm, 10-13
   Guilford Courthouse, 5
   Long Island, 5, 6
   Monck's Corner, 5,
      22-25
   White Marsh, 15, 18-21
   Yorktown, 5, 26-29
Battles of Saratoga,
   5, 13
Benjamin, Sarah Osborn,
   26-29
Boston Tea Party, 4

calvary, 22
Canada, 10, 25
Cornwallis, Charles, 29

Darragh, Lydia, 14-17
Declaration of
   Independence, 5, 6-7

Howe, William, 14-17, 21

King George III, 4, 8,
   9, 22, 25

loyalists, 25

Redcoats, 9, 18
Revolutionary War
   cause of, 4
   end of, 4, 5, 29
   key dates of, 5
   start of, 4, 5

spying, 14-17

von Riedesel, Frederika,
   10-13, 29

Waldo, Albigence, 18-21
Washington, George, 6,
   9, 15, 16, 17, 18, 19,
   22, 28